The American Journalists

A TREATISE ON THE LAW OF LIBEL AND THE LIBERTY OF THE PRESS

Thomas Cooper

ARNO
&
The New York Times

Collection Created and Selected
by Charles Gregg of Gregg Press

Reprint edition 1970 by Arno Press Inc.

LC# 78-125688
ISBN 0-405-01665-4

The American Journalists
ISBN for complete set: 0-405-01650-6

Reprinted from a copy in
The New York Public Library

Manufactured in the United States of America

A

TREATISE

ON THE

LAW OF LIBEL

AND THE

LIBERTY OF THE PRESS;

SHOWING THE ORIGIN, USE, AND ABUSE OF THE LAW OF LIBEL:

WITH COPIOUS NOTES AND REFERENCES TO AUTHORITIES IN GREAT BRITAIN AND THE UNITED STATES:

AS APPLICABLE TO INDIVIDUALS AND TO POLITICAL AND ECCLESIASTICAL BODIES AND PRINCIPLES.

BY

THOMAS COOPER, M. D. L. L. D. AND

President of Columbia College in S. C.

New-York:

PRINTED BY G. F. HOPKINS & SON,

No. 44 Nassau-street.

....

1830.

Columbia, 11th Dec'r, 1829.

Dear Sir,

Your note relating to my manuscript of the Law of Libel and the Liberty of the Press, has been received; and the manuscript will herewith be handed to you. I pray you to peruse it without any of the partiality of friendship, and to dispose of it as you may judge best.

From yours,
With great respect and regard,
THOMAS COOPER.

The hon'ble John L. Wilson.

Charleston, 24th Dec'r, 1829.

The manuscript, my dear Sir, which you have been pleased to transmit for my perusal, and to confide to my discretion, has been perused with the utmost pleasure, and, I may add, with instruction. It is, in my opinion, eminently calculated to be useful in this country, and at this juncture.

With this belief, it would be criminal to withhold it from the public.

Very respectfully,
Your friend and s't,
JOHN L. WILSON.

To Thos. Cooper, M. D. &c.

PREFACE,*

BY AN UNKNOWN FRIEND OF THE AUTHOR.

FROM the earliest history of civilization to the present day, a doctrine has been sedulously inculcated, and perseveringly enforced, that certain subjects are too momentous for discussion; that the opinions of our rulers respecting them are to be adopted with reverential submission, and without farther inquiry; that they are to be approached (in the language of an English dignitary, the present Bishop of London,) "with humble prostration of the intellect," and that the public discussion of doctrines that ought to be received implicitly on the authority of our superiors, is itself a crime.

* The side of the question maintained in the following pages, was first maintained abstractedly, so far as I know, by JOHN MILTON, in his Areopagita, or treatise on free and unlicensed printing. Afterwards, by ANTHONY COLLINS, in the preface to his Grounds and Reasons of the Christian Religion; 1724. Next, by THOMAS COOPER, of Manchester, in page 167 of a volume of Tracts, printed 1787. Then by the Reverend Mr. ROBERT HALL, in an Apology for the Freedom of the Press; London, 1821. Latterly, with great force of reasoning, in an Essay on the Formation and Publication of Opinions; second edition, London, 1826. And very recently, though incidentally, in an able pamphlet, published in New-York, entitled the Demurrer, by THOMAS HERTTELL, 1828. The author of the present tract has adopted the views on the necessary, not voluntary, character of belief; first distinctly, though briefly, stated by Mr. Locke, but very forcibly urged in the Essay on the Formation and Publication of Opinions.

All this has not only been taught, but enforced by the pains and penalties of the law, by politicians and theologians from time immemorial. It is the prevailing opinion among that class of men, at this moment, throughout Europe: in many parts of these United States it is the law of the land. The courtly conformity of the bench and the bar to the wishes of government in England, has made it so in that country; and the dread of innovation among the profession in many of our States, has induced them to pay more than a reasonable comity to the political and theological maxims of British jurisprudence. The great mass of the people too, in every age and in every country, has been urged to adopt this manifest heresy against their own rights and interests.

But PUBLIC OPINION has awakened from her long slumber; and the questions have gone abroad—What are the motives and designs of those who would prohibit discussion? Is it from a love of truth that inquiry is forbidden? What are the classes of society that consider discussion as dangerous? And a strong suspicion now prevails, that the human intellect has been kept in fetters, by men who have boldly assumed superior wisdom, that their dictates might pass without inquiry—men who professedly deal in concealment, darkness, and mystery, and who fatten upon human ignorance. Is not this true in a manifest degree, of all the governments and establishments of the old world? It is in fact so here; and it will require constant vigilance among the enlightened part of our own community, to prevent this intellectual tyranny from overrunning the land.

There are, even at this moment, and among ourselves, who deem it nothing less than treason or sedition, to suggest a doubt of the infallibility of our ancestors, or to investigate the principles or tendencies of the constitution under which we live! as if we had not a right to follow the example they set us! as if the world decreased in knowledge as it increased in experience! as if change could never be wrought by time! as if infallibility had ever been the attribute of humanity! as if the circumstances of the present and of all future ages, in all their details, and in all the change of interests arising from them, were clearly foreseen and provided for by the men who lived half a century ago! Too many of us, however, feel that it is not so. And who is to prohibit us from assuming, for our own sakes, that liberty of investigating the doctrines of our ancestors, which those wise and able men so boldly and successfully assumed with theirs?

Those who are averse to have their own opinions examined, are manifestly actuated more by attachment to their own tenets than to truth. They arrogate for themselves a privilege which they deny to their neighbor; and they suggest the suspicious inquiry—Is there any concealed interest in the back ground that causes discussion to be dreaded and opposed?

I intend, therefore, upon the present occasion,

to maintain the RIGHT OF FREE DISCUSSION, in its fullest extent: as applied to any and every question, opinion, or doctrine, political, theological, moral, metaphysical, or philosophical, within the widest range of human inquiry: and I trust I shall show, that the cause of truth, and the interest of the public, requires the free and full exercise of the right now claimed: and that in all times and places, those who have been so anxious to throw fetters around the human intellect, have had no other motive for so doing, than to keep the persons, and the property of their fellow men, more completely within their own control.

Let it be remembered, that whatever may be the *expediency* of admitting untrammelled discussion in its utmost latitude, it is the RIGHT I now claim. I am under no obligation to my neighbor for tolerating my opinions, however erroneous he may deem them. Do I not tolerate his? Who made *him* a judge between us? or invested him exclusively with the power of distinguishing truth from error? I claim the same privilege in that respect that he does; nor can I discover his title to the required infallibility.

I know not one subject within the whole compass of human inquiry so important as the present. In the whole range of human investigation, there is not one question wherein human happiness is so deeply involved. It lays at the very root of all national improvement, and all personal security. There is no such thing as truth without full and free discussion; for who has a right to assert that any doctrine is true, upon a one-sided discussion of it? The mistakes that have prevailed upon this subject among politicians and theologians, have given rise to the exercise of more vexatious interference, of more tyranny, of more rancorous hate, more deliberate and legalized cruelty and murder, than any other source of human misery, from the commencement of civil society to the present day. The page of history is filled with details of persecution: civil history with the wars of political rulers, upon those who have been bold enough to advocate the rights of the people: and ecclesiastical history with the wars of contending sects, and the merciless punishments inflicted upon all who have dared to hint a dissent from established error. The law, unfortunately, has always been retained on the side of power: laws have uniformly been enacted for the protection and perpetuation of power; and the people themselves have been worked upon by their enemies, to treat with persecuting cruelty and ferocious hatred, their most honest, their boldest, and their best friends. It is true, the love of power and the love of wealth have been at the bottom of these persecutions; but they have been publicly and ostensibly based upon the fallacy, that *opinion or belief is an act of the will:* that any man may believe as he pleases; and therefore, as his belief is a voluntary act, and depends upon himself, he is punished' for not believing what his superiors tell him he ought to believe. It is my business, therefore, to show that opinion or belief is an act, *not* of the will, but of the understanding; that no man can believe what he pleases, or what others please. That opinion or belief, in every possible case, depends not on the good will and pleasure of the man, but on the evidence to which he has actually had access, and on that only. So that (in the language of Mr. Brougham) a man is no more answerable for what he really believes,—for the features of his opinion, than for the features of his face: both the one and the other are formed by circumstances not within his voluntary control; and it is as unjust to punish him for the one as for the other.

The wise men to whom we owe the constitutions under which we live, did much to set free the press from the control of the law: much, indeed, do we owe them for the benefits they have conferred. But the leven of ancient prejudice is still at work among the mass of society, even in this land of freedom; and in many cases the constitution of the country guarantees a right, which the want of general information renders unpopular in its exercise. Those who love truth because it is necessary to human improvement, ought to unite in their efforts to unfetter it.

I wish it to be distinctly understood in the outset of this inquiry, that I advocate no sect, no creed, political or theological. I enlist under the banners of no party. My design is to show that each and every of them ought to have fair play.

I seek only to establish those principles whic are best calculated to bring truth to light, wherever she is to be found. It will be seen that no political ruler is deserving of confidence who hesitates to meet inquiry; that no form of government is a good one that will not bear investigation; no religion is worth supporting that needs any other support than its own intrinsic evidence. Every politician, every member of the clerical profession, ought to incur the reasonable suspicion of being an interested supporter of false doctrine, who becomes angry at opposition, and endeavors to cast an odium on free inquiry. Fraud and falsehood only dread examination. Truth invites it. Public discussion is the spear of Ithuriel; the fiend Imposture starts up, trembling at its touch.

It is a prevailing opinion, that some doctrines are so important in politics, and others so sacred in religion, that no public discussion of them ought to be allowed. If this opinion were well founded, then would all the persecution that has ever been practised in the world be justified. For, if it be part of the duty of civil magistrates to prevent the discussion of such doctrines, they must, in so doing, act on their own judgments, as to the *nature and tendency of doctrines*. Consequently they must have a right to prevent the discussion of all doctrines which they deem improper for discussion. This right they must exercise in the only way in which civil power is capable of exercising it; that is, by inflicting pains and penalties on all who oppose what our governors deem sacred doctrines ; or who maintain what they are pleased to call pernicious opinions. So that the opinions of our political rulers become the established test of truth. In Mahomedan countries, therefore, magistrates would have a right, and it would be their bounden duty, to silence and punish all who oppose the divine mission of Mahomet, or the inspired character of the Koran. The like is true of the doctrines of transubstantiation, the real presence, the worship of the virgin Mary, &c. in popish countries ; and the doctrines of the trinity, the atonement, unconditional election, and reprobation, in protestant countries. All such prohibitory and penal laws are right, if the prevailing opinion, which I now controvert, is right : and papists and protestants very properly burned each other at the stake, alternately, and may justly continue to do so when they happen to have the power. This is the necessary, undeniable consequence of the doctrine that we, or the governors of a country, wherever that may be, have a right to punish in any manner those who maintain what may be considered as pernicious opinions in religion or government. How many people will agree in theory, that the prevailing notion is a mistaken one, and yet make an exception in practice, in favor of their own opinions! In this mutual conflict of hatred and revenge, which for so many centuries has disgraced the population of Europe, what has become of truth while each of the contending parties have indulged their rancor under her sanction, and pretended to fight under her banners!

In reality, civil power has nothing to do with such matters. Speculative opinions are best left to fight out their own harmless battles by means of a free press. They are never dangerous to the community but when the magistrate takes a side. But who constituted our civil governors arbitrators of opinion? Or when have they ever interfered but to increase the acrimony of the disputants, and misemploy their own authority? Indeed, the opinion I have just advanced and adopted for myself, is strenuously maintained in every nation under heaven, as to the application of the civil power to doctrinal points, in every other country but their own. Does any calvinist, in Europe, scruple to allow that laws for the protection of popery, are inexpedient and unjust? Does any papist in Spain or Italy, pretend that the adherents of Martin Luther, John Calvin, or Faustus Socinus, ought to be tolerated? It is, indeed, tyranny, superstition, idolatry, and absurdity, that civil power obviously supports in every country in Europe, at the present moment, under the pretence of protecting regular government, social order, and sacred truth. It is sufficient for me to appeal to the holy alliance in proof of the assertions I have advanced, who have put a padlock on the lips of every man subjected to that detestable combination. Would not, therefore, perfect neutrality be the greatest blessing? Would not the interests of truth gain unspeakably, were all the rulers of States to aim at nothing but defending their people from enemies without, and keeping the peace within? To me it seems, that they would act wisely and to the full extent of their reasonable jurisdiction, if they considered themselves bound to take care not of the *future* but the *present* interest of men; not of their souls and their faith, but of their persons and their properties; not of any ecclesiastical, but of secular matters only; and to consider *actions* and not *opinions* as the proper objects of their control. I wish I could say that these remarks were in no degree applicable to our own country, and our own times, and to proposals of very recent date, though not of recent origin.

The supposed dangerous or immoral tendency of doctrines, which is so often urged as a reason for prohibiting them, is either *avowed and direct, or presumed and inferred only*. But who will dare in any society to avow doctrines that imply in themselves, openly and directly, a breach of morality? Who defends robbery, murder, adultery, fraud, or falsehood? The indignation of society would at once frown down the mad and harmless attempt.

"But the tendencies and consequences of the doctrines we complain of (it is said) are subversive of good government, of religion, and morality?"

Are they so? And what polemic, in politics,

religion, ethics, or metaphysics, has not charged his adversary with these consequences and tendencies? Does not the holy alliance say the same of the British latitude of discussion? Does not the British monarchist make this a serious objection to American republicanism? Do not the various parties in our own republic make the same outcry against each other? Do not papists and protestants, calvinists and arminians, trinitarians and unitarians, fatalists and freewillers, continually exclaim against each others' opinions as licentious and dangerous? Christianity itself, at its first introduction, did not escape this most common accusation. Its professors were called atheists, because they opposed the Pagan superstitions and idolatry. Hence, Christianity was long regarded as a pernicious enthusiasm. The same objection was urged against the protestant reformation, and will be urged against every real reformation. If, therefore, legislators may enact laws prohibiting the propagation of all doctrines in which they think they discern dangerous tendencies, the gates will be thrown open for every species of persecution. There will be no doctrine, however true or important, which will not, in some country or other, be subjected to civil penalties. Can we forget the imprisonment of Galileo, or the dangerous tendency of astronomical truth? Do you want a catalogue of valuable books,—of publications that do honor to the age? I refer you to the *index expurgatorius*.

I think I may safely appeal to all who hear me: are there not many good and wise men—men who do honor to society, within our own immediate knowledge, who rank among the heterodox as well as the orthodox; good and wise men, who are papists, calvinists, trinitarians, methodists, unitarians! What more can we fairly require, than that in all the practical relations of life, our neighbor should be a good man?

In fact, the bad tendency of merely speculative opinions, however widely they may differ from those that generally prevail, is an imputation, often made from ignorance and inattention to matter of fact, but more generally as the poisoned weapon of malignant controversy. It is an imputation always resorted to by the adherents of political and theological orthodoxy: by those whose interest it is, that all errors and abuses should pass quietly, sub silentio. No wonder such men should fervently pray against all false doctrines, heresy and schism! Look around you, my friends, and observe how many wise and estimable men, whose conduct in society is irreproachable, differ from you and from each other on controverted points of politics and religion: so it always has been, and so it probably will ever be. Let us measure each other by the general tenor, not of our opinions, but of our conduct. However erroneous our speculative opinions may seem to others, or theirs to us, there is no danger but all of us will feel the indispensable importance of those plain rules of morality without which society cannot exist. Let the laws regulate our *actions*, which are within the power of regulation; and leave our *opinions* alone, because no external force can produce or destroy them. Quiet, unmolested, continued discussion, is ultimately the most efficient peacemaker.—Amidst our own innumerable sects and parties of all descriptions, have we not always found it so? Governments, says *Dr. Jortin*, in the admirable preface to his ecclesiastical history, do not compel men to *think* alike, for that is impossible, but to *say* they do. They compel heretics to become liars and hypocrites, for the good of their souls, and the peace of the church! Et, ubi solitudinem faciunt, pacem appellant. They exterminate till the land is a desert, and they call it peace!

In a similar spirit of compulsion, are the decisions of the British, and of many courts in this country, on the admissibility of testimony. All such laws and decisions as cast a stigma of reproach or disability on any man for his opinions on theological subjects, whatever they may be, are laws and decisions in favor of the alliance between church and state; they operate for the encouragement and protection of legal falsehood and hypocrisy. They stigmatize conscientious veracity as among the worst of crimes, and punish it accordingly. They tacitly admit the temptation to utter preliminary falsehood, as the best possible test of the inclination to tell truth. They take for granted, that a disposition to speak truth fearlessly and at all hazards, is a sure sign that the person in question is unworthy of all belief! And by the courtesy of the country, in many States, this is called LAW.

Suppose medicine or chymistry had been regarded as subjects of legislative control, and heresies in doctrine had been forbidden by law, a century ago, what would they have been now? Suppose success had attended the recent efforts to put astronomy, physiology, zoology, and geology under interdict,—what improvement would have been made in them? Can knowledge be advanced by loading her with the drag-chain of ignorance and suspicion? Can we be made wiser by half-information, or see more clearly in proportion as our field of vision is obstructed?

If the government of a country has a right to control the publication of opinions, and to interfere with public discussion, let us examine what class of opinions they are likely to interfere with, and whether the public interest will be promoted by their interference.

It is manifest, that in politics, the governing powers will prohibit, if they can, every discussion that will tend to diminish their own influence, or lead the people to think too accurately as to the foundations of assumed authority, or the extent, the use, or abuse of any authority whatever, entrusted or assumed. So it always has been, and so it always will be on the known principles of human nature. Did not the *sedition law* of this republican country, passed on this very principle, under the influence of a former president, and sanctioned by judges of the supreme court, creatures of presidential appointment, enact and decide, that to publish any thing even *tending* to bring the officers of government into disrespect with the people, was an offence punishable by indictment? If such mistakes could take place in republican America, where else are the people safe under a supreme controlling power over the discussions of the press? If farther proof be wanting of the nature of the questions which such a power would prohibit or control, I refer to the state trials in particular, and generally to the melancholy, but most ample catalogue of indictable opinions, which are embraced in England by the abominable law of libel in that country, political and theological. A list of offences most ample, indeed, and most disgraceful. Nor would it be a hard task to show that the offender, in every case of every description, was actuated by honest motive, and deserved well of his country for the very offence of which he was convicted. It is that black list of enormities, committed by the servile slaves of power, that tempts every well informed man, when he hears of a court of justice in Great Britain, to exclaim against the misnomer.

The power contended for, therefore, is an unsafe power; whether you consider it in theory, or in the detestable mass of facts, which constitute the practice under it. Nor can any friend to this country be otherwise than an enemy to the claim, whether urged in favor of the church or in favor of the state.

Moreover, let us look at the times and places where the government of the country has arrogated the right of control over the press; and we shall find that they are the times and places where despotism and ignorance have most prevailed; while freedom, happiness, and general knowledge have flourished every where, in proportion as the right of public discussion has been more freely permitted and acted upon. For proof of this, look at the liberal practice of Greece and Rome in their republican times. Compare Italy, Spain, France, now, with Great Britain. Look at the rapid progress of improvement in this country. These are cases full in point. Nor is it other than we might reasonably expect beforehand. If general happiness and national prosperity be connected with the general diffusion of knowledge, and if knowledge be the result of freedom of inquiry, then is freedom of inquiry one at least of the main sources of national prosperity.

No class of men will ever suffer, if they can help it, those maxims and tenets to be controverted, which enable them to assume power, to obtain rank and consideration in society, and to live in ease and affluence. Every government is jealous of investigation, in proportion as it has reason to fear it. Every clerical tenet is defended with a pertinacity that increases with the weakness of the argument. The law is always applied to, and then only when the cause is weak. If two boys are fighting, and one calls in a third to his aid, is it not a plain confession that his antagonist is the stronger? Free inquiry, therefore, will be checked, if possible, wherever it is feared; for no other valid reason can exist for checking it; and the attempt to suppress or control it, furnishes incontrovertible proof of its utility and necessity.

Why is it that long experience has compelled us in this country to establish it as a maxim, that no representative shall be called upon *out* of the Legislature, to answer for any opinion or any expression he may have used *in* it? What but our perfect conviction that the most absolute freedom of discussion is necessary to expose mistake or delinquency, and to bring the truth into full light? If this be so in politics, why is it not so in every other case where truth is to be elicited? Can any assignable reason be urged for the practice in one case, that will not apply to all? I know of none.

Indeed, no opinion or doctrine, of whatever nature it be, or whatever be its tendency, ought to be suppressed. For it is either manifestly true, or it is manifestly false, or its truth or falsehood is dubious. Its tendency is manifestly good, or manifestly bad, or it is dubious and concealed. There are no other assignable conditions, no other functions of the problem.

In the case of its being manifestly true, and of good tendency, there can be no dispute. Nor in the case of its being manifestly otherwise; for by the terms it can mislead nobody. If its truth or its tendency be dubious, it is clear that nothing can bring the good to light, or expose the evil, but full and free discussion. Until this takes place, a plausible fallacy may do harm: but discussion is sure to elicit the truth, and fix public opinion on a proper basis; and nothing else can do it.

All these abstract propositions might easily be illustrated by instances of the very harmless nature of much dreaded doctrines. But I abstain from such an illustration, that I may afford no room for apprehension or mistake; or subject myself to the suspicion of being an advocate of opinions, where my real intention in the present essay, is perfect neutrality.

Another branch of this subject I must touch briefly before I close this essay, because it is too important to be omitted.

Is any man accountable for his belief or his unbelief? Can praise or blame, merit or demerit, attach to the one state of mind or the other? I answer unhesitatingly, no, under the limitation about to be stated. He is accountable for the voluntary use, or the voluntary neglect, of evidence reasonably within his power. But the actual effect of evidence on his understanding, is not within the control of his will.

It is a common expression, introduced and sanctioned by daily experience and observation, that the evidence is irresistible; it is impossible to refuse assent to it. Why? Cannot I believe it or not as I please? No: for evidence is not an object of volition; its properties are not within your command or control; it is not addressed to the *will*, but to the *understanding*. An apple and an orange are placed before me; it is not in my power to believe, at pleasure, that the orange is an apple, or the apple an orange. I may obstinately shut my eyes, and refuse to look at them, but can I disbelieve my eyesight? An arithmetical problem is before me,—can I refuse my assent to the assertion that two and two make four?

What mathematician doubts whether the square of the hypothenuse, in a right-angled triangle, be equal to the sum of the squares of the other two sides? What merit or demerit is there in agreeing to these statements? Who thanks me for my assent? What has my will or inclination to do with it?

Suppose clear and undeniable testimony of a fact, probable in itself, were given to a jury, by witnesses well known to them, well acquainted with all the circumstances, of irreproachable character, and fully corroborated by circumstantial evidence; could the jury help believing it? Under the old law, founded on the misconception I am now combating, the court might threaten them with an attaint and imprisonment, as has been repeatedly done in England. They may be induced, if such were the law, as they have been in England, through fear of punishment, to bring in a verdict in opposition to the evidence and to their own convictions. They may belie their own consciences, if they please, for the verdict they pronounce is voluntary. But no threat can alter their real belief. They are compelled, by the constitution of the human mind, to *believe* according to the evidence; but to *utter* the words guilty or not guilty, is an act of the will, and in their power. The state of their understanding, produced by the testimony, remains the same. Their verbal declaration of it, may be true or false, as they please. It may be said these are extreme cases; and they are so. My object is to show in what way, evidence of all kinds, produces an effect upon the understanding; to show, that whether it be convincing or not, depends upon the understanding which is passive, and not upon the will. If the evidence be full and clear, the effect produced will be *conviction;* if doubtful, *hesitation;* if weak, inadequate, and unsatisfactory, *disbelief:* nor is it in our own power to avoid these results. In every supposable case, the operation and effect of evidence, be it good or bad, perfect or imperfect, partial or impartial, is upon the understanding, and not upon the will. It is not in our power to resist the impression it is naturally calculated to produce upon our understandings, such as they are. It is true, *quicquid recipitur, recipitur ad modum recipientis,* upon a well trained and cultivated understanding, preoccupied by no extraneous bias, the effect will be more certain and decided, than on the untutored and ignorant mind of a man unaccustomed to reason. But in the one case, and in the other, the effect, whatever it be, is a necessary effect; over which the will has no control; for the evidence itself, with all its properties, is extraneous to, and independent of the person to whom it is offered.

It is in our power to say, to profess, what we please: it is not in our power to think as we please. Evidence may be counteracted by prejudice, by motives of interest, by party bias, by our previous wishes and inclinations, which prevent it having its full effect: it may fail of its full effect from the prejudice, the ignorance, the dulness, or inattention of him to whom it is offered. But its real operation, be it greater or less, cannot be counteracted by mere volition. Suppose a force unresisted, acts with the power 4: suppose it be resisted by the power 5; still it will act with the power 4, although it be unable to overcome the resistance opposed to it.

If a man therefore be exposed, during the greater part of his life, to the continual influence of motives and evidence on one side of a doctrine exclusively, it is hardly possible that his belief should not become at length so fixed, as to lead him to reject all evidence to the contrary. His creed has become habitual; too deeply associated with all his feelings to be eradicated. This involuntary state of things may be his misfortune; it is no fault.

Let an infant be brought up to middle age at Constantinople: taught by his parents, his tutors, his friends, his neighbors, by all those to whom he looks up as persons of wisdom, honesty, authority, to believe in the divine mission of Mahomet, and the inspiration of the Koran,—can the evidences of Christianity make an impression on such a man? When has it ever happened? The laws of mental association, under which his intellect has been formed, forbid it. Can such a man be blamed for his mistaken opinions? Is he a proper object of punishment? Guilty of rejecting a doctrine whose evidence he has never been permitted to examine!

Let the same case be put as to a Roman catholic, or a calvinistic presbyterian: suppose them, as they usually are, educated in the manner above described; can their creed be considered as a voluntary choice on their part? Suppose them mistaken, are they the subjects of rational blame?

How very few among the Jews, how very few among the Hindoos, have really been converted to missionary Christianity! They have been exposed to one species of evidence exclusively: to the evidence in favor of the religion of their parents, their friends, their country; of all to whom they look up with reverence and affection. All their strongest associations have been intertwined for years with their present belief. This has had its effect upon their understandings, now closed by long habit against any other creed. Is involuntary ignorance like this a subject of punishment? God forbid.

But suppose a man's mind open to conviction; free from opposing motive, or opposing prejudice, and that the evidence on both sides of a controverted point be laid before him, and he is anxious to discover the truth,—is it possible for him not to be convinced by what appears to him the better evidence? Can he believe as he pleases, against the convictions of his understanding? Has he any merit for being convinced by a force of evidence in its nature calculated to convince him? Is he to blame, on the other hand, if the weight of evidence should induce him to hesitate, or be utterly insufficient to produce conviction?

From this view of the subject, it results—

1. That a man's understanding is influenced, whether he will or not according to the force of evidence presented to it.

2. That volition is not the faculty addressed by evidence, which operates exclusively on the understanding. When a man hears with attention, or deliberately peruses a train of argument on a disputed question, he is either convinced, or he remains in doubt, or he disbelieves—states of mind that depend on the goodness or otherwise of his own understanding; and the goodness or otherwise of the arguments employed. Volition has nothing to do with the effect produced.

3. Where there is no volition exerted, there is neither merit or demerit; no room for praise or blame, which can never be applied where the effect is produced whether we will or no. All

actions are indifferent, except as to the intention, volition, or quo animo with which they are performed.

4. Hence, no man can reasonably be deemed an object of punishment, or even of reproach, for the effect produced on his understanding by that evidence to which alone he has had access. If it be partial and imperfect, and he could obtain no other, error is no crime.

5. Criminality can only be predicated where there is an obstinate, unreasonable refusal to consider any kind of evidence but what exclusively supports one side of a question.

If we voluntarily pick out all the evidence that tends to support the opinions we have already adopted, and wish to be true, and wilfully reject all that can be urged on the other side, this conduct, being voluntary, is therefore blameable. But as to the evidence itself, whether it be good or bad, weak or strong, perfect or imperfect, partial or impartial, its operation is on our understandings, and no voluntary exertion can prevent the effect of it. If an argument really appears conclusive to us, we cannot disbelieve it at our own pleasure. It may have to encounter our prejudices, or stronger arguments, as we may deem them, and may not have weight enough to overcome them; but its operation depends on circumstances that mere volition on our part cannot control. Set a weight to act for the purpose of producing any movement, its *mode of action* will be the same whether it be a pound or a hundred weight; whether the resistance it will have to overcome be great or small; whether it be effectual for the purpose, or ineffectual. In all the variety of cases, it will act by its gravity alone; it will neither be electric or magnetic in its operation. So an argument, be it good or bad, addresses itself, never to the will, but always to the understanding; whatever be the obstacles it has to combat, it acts by its intrinsic force alone; and that is extraneous to our volition, and not controllable by it.

6. But as a man's conduct, in this preliminary respect, can only be known accurately to himself, all laws for the punishment of opinion, are acts of injustice and cruelty. All blame thrown upon a man, because his opinions are different from my own, is unjust: he has formed his opinion on such evidence as occurred to him; and I have done the same.

7. This view of the subject leads us to charitable conclusions; to mutual forbearance and toleration. We all of us are in search of truth. It is never desirable to be misled or mistaken. If I be in error, and my neighbor has discovered the truth, it is the necessary result of his having enjoyed better means and opportunities, natural or acquired, than I have. Ought this to be a cause of anger and animosity against me? My want of knowledge is a misfortune, not a crime; and charity should so consider it; provided always that I do not conjoin bad passions, and intolerant behaviour to erroneous opinions.

8. As volition relates to actions only, and not to opinions, praise or blame, merit or demerit, reward or punishment, should be applied to actions only, not opinions. Punishment may produce resentment and hardness of heart, but it can never convince. Am I allowed to confute my adversary by replying to the major of his syllogism by a blow on the head: to his minor by imprisoning his person; or to his conclusion by setting the populace against him, as if he were a mad dog, unworthy of all argument? Yet, how often has this been done! Nay, at this very day, how common is the practice! And how much more common would it be, if public opinion did not show strong symptoms of dislike to persecution, whether for political errors or theological heresies.

9. From this course of reasoning it follows, that errors of the understanding must be treated by appeals to the understanding. That argument should be opposed by argument, and fact by fact. That fine and imprisonment are bad forms of syllogism; well calculated to irritate, but powerless for refutation. They may suppress truth, they can never elicit it. So, for the same reason, are private reproach and public obloquy. They excite and encourage bad feelings on both sides of a disputation, and convince neither party. Am I in error? Confute me, or convince me; but it is useless to employ any weapon for the purpose but argument. If we cannot convince each other, the press is open, let

discussion be free; and in due time, the public will decide rightly between us. That is the ultimate and proper tribunal. Those who treat difference of opinion by terms of reproach, ought not to complain if reproach be retorted. If abuse be employed where argument is called for, it is proof sufficient that the man who degrades himself by abuse, has no better argument to offer.

10. Hence, also, faith or belief, as such, can have neither merit or demerit. It depends on the evidence which has produced it, be that evidence weak or strong. A man who has been taught from his earliest infancy the doctrines of Christianity, and has been carefully drilled into every argument, and had every kind of evidence enforced upon him, whereon the Christian doctrines rest, can have no merit in believing and adopting them. How could he do otherwise? So a Mussulman, or a Hindoo, who from earliest infancy to advanced age, never heard the truth of his own tenets controverted, or any other religion expounded to him, cannot have any demerit, or deserve any punishment, for not being a Christian! How was he to become one? Will it be required of him "to make bricks without straw?"

The criterion of our merit in society, at any rate, is our conduct, not our opinions. The one is within our control, the others are not. This is true of the inhabitants of New-York, or Boston, or London, or Paris, or Constantinople, or Benares. Our *conduct* also is under the control of the laws, which furnish the sanctions of rewards and punishments; but what law can make us *think and believe* as the legislators ordain? How long, how perseveringly, how tyrannically, how cruelly, have legislators and rulers in all ages, and every where, endeavored to make men orthodox according to law? If their intent was to enforce and extend hypocrisy and dissimulation, they have succeeded to their hearts content; but whose *opinions* have they changed? Whose character have they bettered by this feigned and compelled assent? It is no wonder that the clergy of all ages and countries have attached so much importance to what they call *faith:* that is, an implicit, confiding assent to those doctrines which they find it convenient to teach. It is an implicit confidence in the authority of the priesthood—"that humble prostration of the intellect," so much lauded by the present bishop of London. It is a servile frame of mind in the hearer, very convenient, and extremely flattering to the teacher. It dispenses alike with argument and proof; it saves abundance of trouble, and removes innumerable difficulties. But faith grounded upon no evidence, or upon bad evidence, or upon imperfect evidence, is surely any thing but praiseworthy. It is the coal heaver's faith—the *fides carbonaria* of the Roman catholics. But suppose faith to be the result of honest impartial examination, and of full and conclusive evidence; *can* the examiner be any other than a believer; is he not so of necessity?

What merit then has he, for that impression produced on his understanding, which no reasonable and sensible man could possibly reject or avoid ?

But the maxim of orthodoxy is, "he that believeth shall be saved, and he that believeth not, shall be damned." Believe! What? The tenets of their priests; and the more abstruse and mysterious those tenets are, the more he becomes necessary to his credulous flock, and the greater their dependence upon him. Faith, such as the clergy require, is not the assent of the understanding after long and laborious investigations, but that outward and verbal, that ready, unhesitating assent, which is paid to their superior authority, as the representatives and vicegerents of the Almighty. This answers all the purposes of the priesthood: it is accompanied by reverence for their assumed character, by implicit obedience to their commands, and by pecuniary contributions to their ease and comfort. To the clergy, these are of far more importance, than that honest but troublesome independence of spirit which yields no voluntary expression of assent but as the result of the conviction of the understanding. An independence of spirit, extremely obnoxious to priests, because it is extremely unmanageable, although accompanied by the utmost purity and integrity of conduct. Hence, the very inferior light in which "good works" are always placed by the orthodox clergy; insomuch that the article on good works, among the

39 articles of the church of England declares, that if they do not proceed from faith, "no doubt they have in them the nature of sin." Nor in fact is there any difference on this subject between the calvinists and the antinomians. A more dishonest, though successful attempt to bind the human intellect in fetters, has never been made by any other among the various forms of superstition, than by this exaltation of credulity under the denomination of faith.

But although a man cannot be prevented from holding a mischievous opinion, may he not be prevented from publishing it? No: for whether it be mischievous or not, cannot be known till it be published. Nor can it be mischievous if fully discussed; for then its real tendency will be fully exposed. Nor ought such a power to be entrusted to any set of governors, or law makers; for all those publications will be prohibited that are intended, or are likely, to bring public abuses and public delinquents before the people, or to detect and expose mystery, falsehood, and fraud, in any, or in all their forms. I appeal for the truth of this remark to the English law of libel, political and ecclesiastical,—a code of tyranny not yet exploded even in these United States. So far as this power has been exercised heretofore, it has been exercised in support of the interests and the wishes of those who control the press. It is to men who have braved the terrors of the law, and who have voluntarily incurred the risk of self-devotion, that all the improvements in politics, in ethics, in theology, in the sciences, have been owing. From the days of Anaxagoras to those of Galileo; from Harrington, Milton, and Sydney, to the last reported political indictment; from the very commencement of Christianity to the last prosecution for heresy and schism, the persons prosecuted appear to have been actuated, in every instance, so far as I can find, by motives disinterested, honorable, and unimpeachable. This, I think, we are compelled to allow, however we may disagree with their opinions,—opinions which they had as much a right to propose for public consideration as their persecutors had to maintain the converse of them. Grant to our rulers the right of controlling the press, and the empire of mystery, of political tyranny, of ignorance, and of bigotry—the right divine of kings to govern wrong, and the indefeasible character of the holy alliance between church and state will remain for ever unshaken.

Look at the state of national degradation in Spain, Portugal, Italy, where MYSTERY sits enthroned in all her splendors, and in all her terrors; where the pen is powerless, and the press is prostrate; where the gag of tyranny is in the mouth of every patriot! Look at the state of degradation which has seized upon the human intellect in those fine countries, and say to what else can it be ascribed but the slavery of the press, and the interdict of discussion!

In no country under heaven, in no age or time,

have public discussion and the press been as yet perfectly free and uncontrolled. They are not so in Great Britain, or even in this country, and at this time. The law of political sedition, and theological heresy, is not yet fully settled throughout these United States. Even where the law has lost its terrors, public prejudice entrammels discussion; and mere difference of opinion, upon points purely speculative, are sufficient to render a man unpopular, whose motives are honest, and whose conduct is unimpeachable. This is a state of things which the gradual diffusion of information will in time, amend; and nothing else will. A sound and healthy state of public feeling, depends every where on the sound and healthy state of public information; and this can have no other basis but the freedom of public discussion. The motto of our courts of justice belongs to the public on every question submitted to their tribunal; *audi alteram partem.* Let us hear what can be said on all sides; and we will then decide.

If it be desirable to arrive at truth in our inquiries; if it be desirable to avoid error, we must admit every opinion and doctrine liable to doubt or dispute, to be examined on every side, and by all manner of persons who take an interest in the question. Some will bring more, some less talent and knowledge to bear upon it; some will present it to us under one aspect, some under another. At length, this untrammelled license of discussion will put us in possession of the means of deciding accurately, which we can acquire in no other way. In all matters of science, this truth is universally acknowledged, and this course is generally adopted. If in scientific, why not in questions of every other kind?

Error not brought to view, but concealed; error operating not openly, but privately, may be dangerous; for it has no enemy to detect it, and nothing to fear. Publish it, expose it, discuss it, and the vapor is dissipated before the beams of truth.

Look at the despotic countries of the world, and reflect for a moment on the character and motives of those classes of society by whom discussion is forbidden. Reflect on the questions and the doctrines that are thus forbidden in those countries,—is it the interest of the people, or is it the interest of these predominant classes that is consulted by the prohibition? Look again: are not knowledge and power connected; and is not that connexion exemplified beyond the possibility of denial in those countries which have been formerly, and now are, the most prosperous and powerful on the face of the earth? Why are they so? Because knowledge is power; and because the door is closed against knowledge where freedom of discussion is forbidden.

Thanks be to God, all attempts at restraining knowledge, in the present day, are likely to be vain. The spirit of inquiry has gone forth; and no human power can now say, thus far shalt thou go and no farther. Men may still be worried, irritated, goaded, by restraint, or by obloquy, as within these few years, and very recently, they have been, even in Great Britain: mischievous interference may for some time be busy in defence of ancient and established error; but the night of darkness is passing away, and the day star of knowledge has risen upon the world. May its cheering omens be fulfilled!

Such are the views I have thought fit to offer for public consideration on this important subject. If they be erroneous, I hope they will be proved so; for attached as I may be to my own opinions, I hope and trust I am attached to TRUTH still more.

ON

THE LIBERTY OF THE PRESS

AND

THE LAW OF LIBEL.

THE liberty of the press is a phrase in every body's mouth. It forms one of the common-place panegyrics of what are called free governments. It is one of the boasts of those who admire that nonentity the British constitution. It is supposed to flourish particularly in these United States, and to form a distinguishing feature of our American governments. I hardly know in which of them to look for it.

I think there is no question within the whole range of human inquiry, of equal importance to the present one. It is, whether the people should doom themselves to voluntary ignorance, to imperfect knowledge, and place themselves, bound and blindfold, under the guidance of the men who assume to govern them. They have been told by governments and by the priesthood, that the best way of arriving at truth, is by hearing only one side of the question: and they have legislated and acted in conformity to this persuasion. Of late, men begin to suspect that there is no satisfactory access to knowledge upon public questions, but by means of public discussion; and that no limit can be put to the right of discussion, by previous prohibition or by subsequent punishment, that can operate for the good of the people. They require light, and only light. They must judge and act unwisely, if they judge and act in the dark. Shall they bandage their own eyes, that they may see clearer? Open wide the floodgates of information, which the rulers have been so desirous of closing. Then, and then only, will the errors and abuses that have hitherto preyed upon the vitals of society, be swept away by the torrent, and infest us no more.

I do not mean to include in the present investigation, any consideration of what is called private slander; that imputation of conduct or character to an individual, which ought to subject him to punishment, or degrade him in the opinion of his fellow citizens; or that injures him unjustly in his property or profession. This is an offence so seldom committed from public or praiseworthy motives; the imputations are for the most part of so little moment to the public at large; and they furnish so frequent and troublesome a source of litigation, that this tendency to calumny among neighbors, ought to be repressed. Perhaps it may safely be left to a civil action; or under an indictment subject to the rules that prevail in New-York and Massachusetts; and that ought to prevail every where; being, as I am persuaded, the true law upon the subject in England as well as here. The common frailties of human nature require mutual allowance and frequent oblivion, for the sake of mutual charity and the public peace. Where the public are not interested, a needless exposure of those frailties can never be made from a praiseworthy motive. All this is extremely well treated in Judge Waties' argument, in the State of South Carolina vs. Lehre, which I shall have occasion to quote.

I would therefore consider freedom of discussion and the liberty of the press, as relating to questions of a general and public nature only; and where the discussion is expedient to elicit a truth proper for the public to know.

Is it necessary that laws should be enacted to regulate *opinions* of any kind, or the publication of them? Can truth be discovered in any case, if the discussion of it be forbidden, or carried on partially, or under the dread of subsequent punishment? Does there exist any man, or class of men, who are competent and entitled to dictate to their fellow men, upon a doubtful question, what is truth and what is error, or any infallible criterion, by which mankind can judge of truth or error, but the uncontrolled and public discussion of it? When a question has been viewed and canvassed under all its aspects and bearings, and no more remains to be urged on either side, then and then only, can we reasonably decide where the truth lies. Every court of justice knows this. But the history of the world, from its commencement to the present day, in every country without exception, has exhibited two classes of men, who have uniformly endeavored to forbid or trammel public discussion, or to subject it to penal laws. And wo to the offender, whenever the result of the discussion, or the opinions advanced, during the continuance of it, have been hostile to the peculiar power or interest of these two classes, or calculated to expose their errors and abuses. These two classes are *political governors* and the *priesthood* of every persuasion, at every period of time, and in every known country upon earth.

I shall therefore consider,—

1. Whether it be necessary to society, that laws should be enacted to control the discussion or publication of opinions?

2. Whether any laws are necessary to the public interest, either enjoining previous limitation and restraint, or inflicting subsequent punishment, to screen the public characters, conduct and actions of our political rulers, from an open and full discussion of their tendency, motives, and effects?

3. Whether any laws are necessary to the public interest, either enjoining previous limitation and restraint, or inflicting subsequent punishment, in favor of, or against any metaphysical, theological, or ecclesiastical opinion; or in favor or protection of the priesthood of any religion, sect, or denomination; Christian, Jew, or Gentile, Catholic, Protestant, or Pagan.

As to the first question: I hold that it is not necessary to pass any law prohibiting, controling, or punishing the publication of any opinions, or public discussion of any kind; because there can be no control over opinion; which is not a voluntary, but an involuntary act of the mind. We cannot believe as we please: we are compelled by a necessity of our nature to believe according to the evidence presented to us. I cannot believe that a black beaver hat is an ingot of gold. I cannot believe that two added to two make ten. Belief is an effect produced on the understanding; it is not an act of the will. When evidence satisfactory to my mind is offered to me in favor of any proposition, I cannot, at my own will and pleasure, disbelieve the proposition thus evidenced. I may assert that I believe or disbelieve; that is, I may carelessly or hypocritically make an assertion in opposition to evidence, which I cannot actually disbelieve; but my real opinion is beyond my own control: if beyond mine, it is also beyond the control of any law. A penal law may induce me to assert, that black is white; but it cannot make me believe so. That conviction which is the necessary result of the evidence to which my mind has been exposed, whether that evidence be full and complete, or otherwise, is for the time, truth to me; which I am necessarily compelled to acknowledge to myself, whether I like it or not. But may it not be expedient to prevent the publication of opinions in some cases? Does not the public interest require that certain opinions should be suppressed and kept from the public eye? No.

(*a*) The whole history of mankind, from the beginning to the present time, has shown, *that truth does good, and error and imposture produce evil.* Now there are no other means of discovering what is truth and what is error, but by instituting a full, free, unrestrained examination of the question, with all its evidence, and under all its aspects. Truth can never be discovered, nor error and imposture brought to light, by a half discussion, a partial discussion, a one-sided discussion. Truth cannot gain by suppressing and restraining the production of facts and arguments, although error and imposture may. Hence it is, that those who really seek for truth, or who are persuaded that truth is on their side, never object to the fullest liberty of discussion. Error and imposture are always afraid of, and opposed to it.

(*b*) *It is by unrestrained discussion alone, that truth is elicited on every known subject.* It is so with agricultural, manufacturing, commercial, scientific truth; truth in the fine arts, in morals, in the conduct of life. We find it absolutely necessary in our legislatures, and in our courts of law, to leave discussion untrammelled; and even to allow of wanderings from the precise question,—aberration in argument, that can be defended on no other ground. There is no assignable reason, why this practice should not be permitted for the discovery of truth of every description. The reasons that make it proper in one case, make it proper in every other.

(*c*) A proposition may be advanced before the public, either so *palpably wrong* and *outrageous*, that its absurdity or its evil tendency must be seen at once; or it may be so *plausibly wrong*, that it requires much reflection and consideration to discover where the error lies; or it may be so *manifestly* true, as to need little or no discussion, in order to produce conviction.

In the first case, it is manifest, it can do no harm. It need not be prohibited or punished, where its own absurdity prevents the possibility of any injury arising from it.

In the second case, it is necessary that it be published, and openly and fully discussed, to ascertain where the error lies. If it be permitted to work its way in secret, it may prevail from its plausibility, and do mischief. Let it be viewed and examined on all sides, by means of public discussion, and in this, as in every other and former instance, truth will ultimately prevail, and be the more firmly established.

In the third case, publication must do good, and not harm.

(*d*) *If power be given to the government, to say what opinions shall not be held, it amounts to conferring on government the power of declaring what opinions shall be held, and what alone shall be so.* This, indeed, is what governors and the priesthood have always aimed at. They have always endeavored to persuade the people, that it is for their own good they should be kept in the dark. That the people neither ought, nor need to think for themselves, on subjects relating to government or religion. That those who would encroach on the exclusive right of the government to regulate the politics; or the exclusive right of the priesthood to regulate the religion of the country, are unprincipled innovators, who wish only for anarchy and confusion; and tempt the people to intermeddle with subjects which they cannot understand. History shows how very successful these two orders of society have been, in this most daring attempt. Let us see then, on this theory and pretence of the right of government to dictate what the people should hold as true, and what they shall be required to reject as false and dangerous—let us see the kind of opinions likely to be inculcated and prohibited.

And first it may be assumed, that government will take care that no opinions shall be propagated, adverse to their own power or interest, or calculated to throw light on the errors and abuses committed by the class of men who compose the government, by persons high in office. Self defence will be the first object. They will secure themselves as much as possible, in the first instance, by all means of keeping the public in the dark, and suppressing, and prohibiting all investigation of political abuses. The rights of the people must never interfere with the claims and pretensions of those who govern them. Such in *theory* appears likely to be adopted as the line of their conduct. What has been the *fact?* In Austria, Prussia, Russia, France, Spain, Portugal, Italy? Look at the voluminous doctrine of libel in Great Britain; the banishments to Botany Bay, of Muir, Palmer, and Gerard; the numerous prosecutions during the administration of Mr. Pitt, and the trembling jealousy of the ministry of Great Britain, during the whole reign of George the 3d, and until the present administration; whose wise and open conduct has enabled them to defy the test of public investigation. What has Mr. Jefferson, Mr. Madison, or Mr. Munroe lost, by setting the same example here? I have noticed the British doctrine of libel: is not that also, in great part, adopted, even in this country? The words of the sedition law, the favorite act of Mr. J. Adams and his coadjutors, are in exact conformity with the speech of the attorney-general, and the charges of Powis and Allybone, on the trial of the seven bishops; and appear to have been copied from that loyal exposition of the rights and privileges of men in power. Yet has the sedition law been determined to be constitutional by the federal judges under Mr. J. Adams' administration; and the principles of that act are sanctioned in this country, so far as those decisions can support them. So that throughout the United States, every man may be forbidden (out of the walls of congress) to publish any thing that may even *tend* to bring an incompetent, a negligent, or a dishonest public officer into merited contempt! Public opinion has prevented hitherto the re-enactment of the sedition law, and keeps the judicial doctrine of libel in check. But there is nothing else to prevent its revival; and although the officers of government are not screened by a positive act, I see nothing to prevent the undefinable and plastic common law of the parent country from being called in aid; for the sedition law expired without being repealed. Power and patronage are, for the most part, but too successful in giving the tone to public opinion.

The alliance between church and state, by which the former is contented to play the prostitute to the latter, in every government in Europe, has produced a similar effect. The priesthood inculcate from earliest infancy, the necessity of passive obedience to the powers that be; and the latter, in return, prohibit all discussion, by which the privileges and pretensions, the powers and emoluments of the priesthood, and their ecclesiastical and theological doctrines shall be called in question. Between these orders of society, the minds and the bodies of the multitude are kept in fetters. They are taught that discussion is a crime; that it is their interest to be blindfolded and led: and those are represented as anarchists, disorganizers, and the worst enemies of society, who attempt to remove the bandage from the public eye. Hence, the libel code abounds with what are called the crimes of seditious publication, blasphemy, and heresy: and even in many parts of this country, it is held as a crime in law; and it is every where a crime in public opinion, to examine the foundation of those opinions which the clergy are pleased to deliver as the truths of divine inspiration. Vicegerents and representatives of the Almighty, as they assume to be, the ministers of each of the discordant sects, would willingly extend this prohibition, in favor of their own sectarian tenets. Happily for the people, the law has gone no where in this country, beyond the truth of christianity in general. And that is going too far: for our legislators, our judges, and our clergy, are not sufficiently aware, as it appears to me, of the doubts they originate, the handle they give to unbelief, and the manifest injury they do to christianity, by suggesting or proclaiming that it requires any support whatever, beyond the reasonable evidence on which it rests. That is the proper stand for christianity to take, and on that ground it may well be satisfied to stand or fall. We have indeed in this country, dissolved the unholy concubinage between church and state; but it is impossible for an observing man to shut his eyes against the coquetry continually going on between our politicians and the clergy, particularly of late years. We ought to remember, that these classes have never coalesced but for the purpose of duping the people for the common benefit of the contracting parties.

In the *second* place, under this branch of the argument, if power be given to what is usually called the government of a country, to say what opinions may be published, and what opinions shall be punished, the whole knowledge, talent, and intellect of the country, is under the absolute guidance and control of its political rulers: and the more it is so, the worse is the government of the country, the lower is the grade of intellect among the mass of the people, and the greater are the obstacles to public prosperity. That such is the case all over the world, I appeal to the present state of all the European governments; wherein, the national force, energy, and effective power, is in exact proportion to the permitted freedom of the press. The present enlightened ministry of Great Britain, are fully aware of this most important truth; and happily for that country, act in conformity to it. It is not that the liberty of exposing, for instance, the errors and abuses of the political system, or of the church establishment, operates as any immediate cause of the preponderance of Great Britain in the politics of Europe; but this it is—that energy of intellect is increased, as the field of its exertion is extended; and where all the people are excited to intense reflection and incessant discussion, upon every subject of human interest, the power of the mind must in such a country, receive continual and unbounded accession of strength and energy. Such a people must be, as they are there, a superior people.

In the *third* place, under this head of argument, if government be permitted to exclude any questions from public discussion, it must be because the government deems that they cannot be discussed consistently with the general welfare of society. Hence the sedition law prohibited the discussion of any public question, in such a manner as to bring even by remote tendency, the measures of administration, or the conduct and characters of public officers into contempt with the people: and this, if it can be made so by judicial decision, is in principle, the law of the land at this moment. There was no exception or limitation: the expression was not *undeserved* contempt: if it tended to bring contempt on negligence, weakness, or wickedness; no matter, it was a crime. If the public welfare required such a law, and our governors, for the time being, passed it on that pretence, what prohibitory law may they not pass on a similar pretence? Does not this look like the conferring of despotic power? The punishing of all investigation into its exercise, follows as a necessary consequence. Upon the exercise of this power, under the pretence of the general welfare, there actually exists no control, but the vague and uncertain influence of public opinion,—a check, I allow, of very great importance, in modern days, here, and in England; but too fluctuating for permanent reliance; especially where gag laws may be enacted at pleasure, in aid of court patronage and influence, to bias and control it.

(*e*) Moreover, *one of the highest gratifications of human existence—the most important and efficient stimulus to mental labor*, is the expectation of being able to communicate to our fellow men, the results of our inquiries on questions that we think will interest them, because they have interested us. To have this natural and most useful propensity prohibited and suppressed—to lose the result of our lucubrations—to be deprived of the pleasure and the profit that may arise from ulterior discussion, and to be made liable to punishment for our endeavors to add to the mass of what *we* deem useful knowledge—is indeed to throw a damp on that generous ardor for the improvement of our species, which is the distinguishing ornament of the human character. The embargo thus laid upon the publication of obnoxious opinions, may serve the purpose of men who dread the result of public discussion, and who declare all opinions obnoxious that are so to themselves: but the public ought carefully to inquire how this prohibition is to operate to *their* benefit; while they (the public) are at liberty to adopt or reject the opinions proposed, according to the evidence with which they are accompanied. Again: Who are the advocates of freedom of discussion? The friends of freedom in every other respect. Who are its enemies? Those who subsist by political abuses or by clerical superstition. Look through Europe: is it not so? The constant exclamations of these men against the dangerous consequences that would ensue, if all sorts of opinions were advanced, however detrimental in their consequences to society, have formed an argument against the propagation of truth, and in protection of private fraud, founded upon public ignorance at every period of society. It was used on the first propagation of christianity; it was used at the reformation; it is now in constant employment, kept at hard labor by the defenders of kingcraft and priestcraft, in Spain, Portugal, Italy, France, and Austria. It is an argument nearly worn out, sinking under the task imposed upon it in Great Britain, where it still does infinite mischief. In this country, it is still used with mischievous effect; but is, I hope, fast wearing away. What is the reply to it? Permit all sorts of opinions to be published and discussed, that they may not make their way, like the mole, in underground darkness and privacy; but that their fallacy and ill tendency may be shown and brought forward in open day. In such case, where is the danger? Who will adopt them? Is it any wonder that the advocates of existing abuses should be anxious to throw obstacles in the way of inquiry, when the millions upon millions, who form the great mass of human society, upon whose labors the idlers of all descriptions are fed,—who toil night and day, and scantily subsist on the bare necessaries of life, to supply the splendor and the luxuries of kings, courtiers, and priests, seem born but for this purpose; and would be roused to energy, and break the bands, which their taskmasters have imposed, if the press were really uncontrolled? In that case, what would become of from 35 to 40 millions of dollars annually paid to the clergy of all descriptions in Great Britain? Is there not ten times more attachment to religion here than there? Here, where it is left to its own support, and the clergy rely on the good will and respect of their congregations?

Again: The following passage, from the first article of the 6th number of the Westminster Review, is put so forcibly, that I am tempted to transcribe it, from page 289. "It would be hardy to assert, that to give the right "of pronouncing on libel to a judge, is any thing more "than another name for giving it to the government. "But there are many subjects, and these the most im-"portant of all, on which it is the interest of government, "not that the people should think right, but on the con-"trary, that they should think wrong. On these subjects, "therefore, the government is in perfect surety, if it has "the power to suppress, not merely what are called false "and mischievous opinions, but under that imputation, "great and important truths. It is the interest of rulers "that the people should hold slavish opinions in politics: "it is equally so, that they should hold slavish opinions "in religion. All opinions, therefore, whether in politics "or religion, which are not slavish, the government, if it "dares, will be sure to suppress. It is the interest of "rulers, that the people should believe all their proceed-"ings to be the best possible. Every thing, therefore, "which has a tendency to make them think otherwise, "and among the rest, all strictures, however well de-"served, government will use its most strenuous exer-"tions to prevent. If these endeavors *could* succeed—if "it could suppress all censure, its dominion, to whatever "degree it might pillage and oppress the people, would "be for ever secured."

"This is so palpable, that a man must be either insin-"cere or imbecile to deny it: and no one, we suppose, "will openly affirm, that rulers ought to have the power "of suppressing all opinions which they may call mis-"chievous—all opinions which they may dislike. Where "then is the line to be drawn? At what point is the "magistrate's discretionary power of suppressing opinions "to end? Can it be limited in such a manner as to leave "him the power of suppressing really mischievous opin-

"ions, without giving him that of silencing every opinion "hostile to the indefinite extension of his power? It is "manifest even at first sight, that no such limit can be "set. If the publication of opinions is to be restrained, "merely because they are mischievous, there must be "somebody to judge what opinions are mischievous, and "what the reverse. It is obvious, there is no certain and "universal rule for determining, a priori, whether an opin-"ion be useful or pernicious; and that if any person be "authorized to decide, unfettered by such a rule, that "person is a despot. To decide what opinions shall be "permitted, and what prohibited, is to choose opinions "for the people; since they cannot adopt opinions, which "are not suffered to be presented to their minds. Who-"ever chooses opinions for the people, possesses absolute "control over their actions, and may wield them, for his "own purposes, with perfect security."

"It thus appears by the closest ratiocination, that there "is no medium between perfect freedom of expressing "opinions, and absolute despotism. Whenever you in-"vest the rulers of the country with any power to sup-"press opinions, you invest them with all power: and "absolute power of suppressing opinions, if it *could* be "exercised, would amount to a despotism far more perfect "than any which has yet existed; because there is no "country in which the power of suppressing opinions, "has ever, in practice, been altogether unrestrained."

It cannot, in the present day, be exercised in any country to the extent claimed by the government; because the extension of knowledge, and the formation of that strong check now termed "public opinion," prevents it. But the right of government, in this respect, is never lost sight of; and is kept up by continual claim.

I conclude therefore generally, that much good and no injury will ensue to the public interest, by permitting the unlimited, unrestrained, unpunished investigation of any and every question of a public character, and of whatever description. The public interest requires that every difficult question should be patiently and deliberately examined on all sides; under every view in which it presents itself: that no light should be excluded; but evidence and argument of every kind, should have their full bearing. It is thus that the doubtful truths of one generation, become the axioms of the next; and that the painful results of laborious investigation and deep thinking, gradually descend from the closets of the learned, and pervade the mass of the community for the common improvement of mankind.

The question here agitated was first discussed by Mr. Anthony Collins, in his discourse on free inquiry, prefixed to his grounds and reasons of the christian religion, in 1724. In 1787, I also had to take up the same abstract question; and as my arguments do not occupy much space, I shall repeat them here. (Tracts, p. 169.)—It is in all cases whatever, expedient that an opinion of supposed importance and imagined to be true, should be subjected to public investigation. Such an opinion must be true or false: if false, it must be clearly and evidently so; or plausible but fallacious reasons may be urged in its defence. Let us suppose it true: then,—

1. It is always more expedient that truth should be propagated than error: long experience, throughout the whole history of literature, has settled this beyond the reach of doubt: but if the truth be suppressed, the error is, in fact, propagated.

2. Although some temporary inconvenience might arise from the propagation of a truth, yet this is the case with some of the most important and useful truths we are acquainted with: hence, this argument would prove too much.

3. Whatever inconveniences might arise from the publication of an important truth, like all other inconveniences, they cure themselves, in the natural course of things; so that the ultimate result of any truth must be purely beneficial.

4. The making known a truth is, of itself, a certain good: the inconvenience that may result from it, is problematical only. The circumstances should be very strong that are to induce the suppression of a certain good, through fear of a possible evil.

5. It is a settled point, that we are not to argue against the use of a thing, from the possibility of its being abused: for to what good thing will not this objection apply?

6. Among the innumerable experiments that have been made on the propagation of truth, what instance can be produced wherein more good than harm has not resulted from its extension? Our object in seeking truth, is to increase the sum of human happiness. Can error lead us to it?

7. The argument against the expediency of divulging an opinion, although it be true, from the possibility of its being perverted, has been so much hackneyed, and has served so often as the last resort to the confuted abettors of political and ecclesiastical tyranny, in particular, that every man of literature, who has attended to the history of any important opinion, ethical, theological, or political, rejects it, as the mark of a bad cause,—as the last refuge of retreating error.

8. This has been the case so notoriously, that the legislature of every nation in Europe, though in general well disposed toward every restriction on civil and religious liberty, has been under the necessity, in the present advanced stage of knowledge, of relaxing its former severity toward the propagators of new opinions. Finding in the first place, that the mind of every man of sense and spirit, revolts at the restriction: and in the second place, that many opinions, formerly regarded as most dangerous and fallacious, have been found by experience, to be well founded and beneficial.

Hitherto I have argued on the supposition that the opinion objected to, is the true one: but you suppose it false. Then,—

1. If it be clearly and evidently false, so as to need no refutation, the reasons fail for objecting to its publication: for by the supposition, it can do no harm.

2. But suppose plausible and ingenious arguments may be urged in its defence: still all the preceding arguments will hold good, with respect to the person who has adopted the opinion; because every man must ultimately think for himself; and not another for him: and although he judge wrong, yet an erroneous conscience is universally considered as obligatory. So that if the preceding arguments are of weight, he is morally bound to adhere to the opinion he has adopted.

3. As truth will always bear discussion, there is no doubt of a fallacy being at last refuted, if it be promulgated; as it is in all cases, easier to defend truth than error. But if this discussion of a false opinion be prohibited, how can it be refuted?

4. The more strictly a false opinion is concealed or suppressed, the less likely is the true opinion to be known. Many an important truth is more extensively propagated by the discussion of its opposite error.

5. Where, from the supposed inexpediency of publishing it, a plausible but fallacious opinion is concealed, it is far more likely to do harm than if it were known; because, among those who incline to the true opinion, many will not embrace it firmly, on account of the opposing plausible arguments: while many will incline to, or adopt the fallacy on the strength of such arguments, which are not refuted, because they are withholden from public discussion.

6. There can be no discussion without a false opinion and a true one, as the subject matter. It is a known fact, from universal literary history, that the discussion of any opinion, generally brings out many important truths collaterally, which would never have been known or attended to, if the discussed fallacy had not been advanced. From this source alone, I should have no doubt of proving,

that the promulgation of every false opinion on subjects of importance, has been upon the whole, productive of much more good than harm. Examine the history of the reformation with this view: the undisguised claims of the popish clergy, occasioned an examination into the character of those claims: and that brought on the impulse given to the human intellect, by the ardent and manifold discussions of that eventful period.

Such are the chief arguments on which I found the expediency of publishing any and every opinion on subjects of importance, whatever may be its real or supposed tendency. *Magna est veritas et prævalebit.* Indeed, if I were asked what opinion, from the commencement of history to the present day, has been productive of the most injury to mankind? I should answer without hesitation, *the inexpediency of publishing sentiments of supposed bad tendency.* It is this opinion, principally, that has filled Europe with bloodshed, almost unremittingly, for 17 centuries; for it is this opinion that has induced the tyrannical interference of the civil power, not only in political discussions, but in questions of mere theoretical controversy; and punished men, without number, for supposed mistakes in matters of opinion, whose lives and manners were innocent and irreproachable: as if opinions might be adopted or rejected at pleasure, and any deviation from the prescribed standard was a crime. The governors of the people, in every country upon earth, have, during this long period, repeated with indefatigable perseverance, the bloody experiment of dragooning their subjects into silence and uniformity. Thank heaven! repeated disappointments, and more extended knowledge, have considerably relaxed their efforts, especially in this country, (England.) I hope the day is not far distant, when it will be considered as an axiom in politics, that uniform good conduct is, of itself, quite enough to constitute a good citizen; and that ACTIONS alone, and not OPINIONS, are the proper objects of a magistrate's control. Such were my sentiments in 1787, and my subsequent experience has only served to confirm them.

Having assigned my reasons why unrestrained and unpunished discussion should be allowed as a general principle, and extended to every subject of controversy without exception, I wish to consider more particularly the class of subjects that have given rise to the LAW OF LIBEL in England and in this country, as relating to publications; first of *political*, and next of a *religious* character. If I show that the whole system of the law of libel, in political questions, is based upon the necessity of shutting out all argument and inquiry as to the character and conduct of men in high office—all investigation of errors and abuses in the laws or government of a country; that the whole tendency of the law of libel is to deprive the people of the means of information as to the extent of their own rights and privileges, and the infringements made upon them by the bad intentions, mistakes, or misconduct of their public servants; that the manifest effect, as well as design of the law of libel, is to blind the eyes of the people, and not to dispense, but withhold useful information,—I say, if I show this, satisfactorily, to the mind of a reasonable man, I assign sufficient cause to abolish the whole of this iniquitous system. If I show further, that the judges, as a body of men, have, with few exceptions, played into the hands of government, and struggled to make their decisions conformable to the interest and wishes of "the powers that be," and that the whole of the law of libel is neither statute law, nor common law, but judge-made, bench-enacted law, iniquitously imposed upon the people, and countenanced by the political rulers of the country, because it is a system subservient to their interest and pretensions, and calculated to obstruct the prying eyes of public inquiry,—I shall assign cause enough for the representatives of the people to prevent the law of libel from being in force hereafter, so far as political investigations are concerned.

If I make out the same case by the same train of reasoning, as to ecclesiastical and theological questions, and show the absurd inveteracy of the priesthood against all investigation, which might endanger any of their tenets, or jeopardise any of their interests; that from the beginning to the present day, they have struggled with might and main to establish the reign of ignorance and imposture; and that the judges of the land have lent themselves in support of the claims, and aided in confirming the views of the priesthood, by placing religion on the basis of public ignorance,—I shall have a right to draw a similar conclusion, as to the law of libel, ecclesiastical as well as political.

The restrictions on the press, are more despotic in every part of Europe than in England. If, therefore, I deduce my examples from British law and British practice, I shall argue from the instance most favorable to the opinions I oppose, and most applicable to the history and circumstances of our own country. I shall endeavor to do this.

There are two late digests of the English law of libel, both dedicated to Lord Ellenborough, and of approved repute at the English and American bar: the one by Mr. Starkie, and the other by Mr. Holt: Starkie's Treatise on the Law of Libel, 8vo. London, 1813; Holt on the Law of Libel, with a reference to American cases, by A. Bleecker, Esq. New-York, 1818; which can be consulted: and which, with the State Trials and some late reports, will suffice for all the facts and cases I shall have occasion to cite.

Libel has been defined by Lord Coke, and after him by all the compilers, viz.: Hawkins, Holt, Starkie,—*any publication that tends to provoke a breach of the peace.* But this will not apply to one half the cases adjudged to be libel; and it will apply to innumerable cases that have not been so. A bottle of Madeira may have that tendency: a young lady, courted by several suitors: religious discussions have produced more breaches of the peace, and more murders, legal and illegal, than any other cause. For the legal extent of *tendency*,—see the late case of Hunt vs. Bell. 1 Bingh. Rep. 1. 1822.—Some person with equal truth and wit, has defined libel to be,—any thing that hurts the feelings of any body.

The doctrine of libel has been decided to extend;—

1. To any thing written concerning the affairs of the government, without special license.—3 State Trials, Hargrave's ed. p. 57; 4 St. Tr. 304. This point, however, has been tacitly given up in practice.

2. Against the state or constitution.—Holt on Lib. ch. 5.

3. Any thing *tending* to bring the measures of government into hatred or contempt; whether deservedly or not, cannot be made a question.—Attorney-General, in the trial of the 7 Bishops, 4 St. Tr. 304; 5 St. Tr. 527; Tutchin's case per Holt—per Lord Ellenborough, in Cobbet's case, 1804—per Chase and Peters, in Cooper's case, under the Sedition Law, 1800.

4. The same against any officer of government. Ut sup.

5. Against parliament.—Holt on Libel; Owen's case, 11 St. Tr. Append. 197; Stockdale's case.

6. Against courts of justice, or impugning their decisions; that is, in the adopted phrase, affronting the public justice of the nation.—3 St. Tr. 505. 517; 1 St. Tr. 333; 2 Term Rep. 199, per Buller and Ashurst.

7. Against persons in high station generally: by qui tam action under the stat. Scand. Magn.

8. Against magistrates of any description.—St. Tr. ubi. sup. even a dead magistrate: for it is a libel against government that never dies. This is one of Lord Coke's Star Chamber law fictions.—5 Co. Rep. 125.

9. Against the revolution of 1688.—Starkie on Libels, 508.

10. Against the law, or laws.—Ib. 506.

11. Against hereditary right.—Ib. 509.

12. Against persons dead and buried.—Lord Coke, in the case de lib. famosis, 5 Rep. 125; Rex vs. Topham, 4 T. Rep. 126; Rex vs. Critchley, Hil. 7. Geo. 2; Case of Libel on the deceased Lord Cowper.

13. Against morality and public decency.

14. Against the law of nature.

15. Against the law of nations. Libel on foreign potentates.—Chev. D'Eon's case; Vint's case, for a libel on the Empress of Russia; Peltier, for a libel on Buonaparte, defended by Sir James Macintosh.

So much for political libels. In these cases, it is taken for granted, according to the usually received law and definition of libel, that the fictitious personages, the moral entities, (as Puffendorf calls them,) the imaginary beings, entes rationis, called *the Government: the Constitution: the State: Hereditary Right: the Law: the Law of Nature: the Law of Nations*. &c. &c. being very irritable and quarrelsome personages, may be excited to commit a breach of the peace, in revenge for being libelled; for libel is only indictable, as tending to a breach of the peace. These are among the hundred fictions of law, that common sense stares at with astonishment.

16. But libel may be against *religion* in general; and therefore against the catholic religion: for Prisot's Opinion, Year Book, 34 Hen. 6. fol. 38. & 40. Anno 1458. on which (by a gross mistake or grosser fraud) the whole doctrine of religious libel rests, was given long before the reformation.

17. A fortiori, in these our days, against the protestant religion.

18. Against the Christian religion, as by law established. —Holt on Libel; People vs. Ruggles, 8 Johns. Rep. 290; Act of Pennsylvania, 1800; Act of Massachusetts, 1782; Act of New-Jersey, 1796. What constitutes the Christian religion, has never been settled and determined in any law book, by any decision, or even in any treatise of religion, within the course of my reading. Let a Catholic,

a Protestant, a Trinitarian, Arian, Sebellian, Calvinist, Universalist, Unitarian, sit down and agree in a definition, if they can.

19. Against the character of Jesus Christ.—Woolston's case.

20. Against the doctrine of the Trinity, by act of W. 3. now I believe repealed.

21. Exposing any part of the holy scriptures to denial, contempt, or ridicule; as the pentateuch.—Peter Annet's case, Hilary, 2 Geo. 3.

22. Any thing in derogation of the book of common prayer; as in Keach's case, 1664. Or against infant baptism; as in Barth. Legat's case, James I.; Vid. Append. to 6th vol. of State Trials.

23. Or against the Nicene or Athanasian creeds.—Hone's case of parodies, before Lords Ellenborough and Abbot. In our American liturgy, we have struck out the latter of these creeds.

24. Libel may be committed against private persons.

All this long list is an encroachment on the common law, under the construction which the occupants of the British bench have given to it. The law of England really, is what the law of this country is, as laid down by Judge Parsons, General Hamilton, and Judge Kent: nothing is a libel which is written *from good motives and for justifiable ends:* and to show this, the truth of the facts charged as libellous, may be given in evidence; and this, whether against public measures, public officers, or private citizens.

The laws against libelling public officers and great men (læsæ majestatis) were enacted and enforced under Sylla, Julius Cæsar, Augustus, Tiberius, and Domitian. (Holt.) The Laws de Libellis famosis, I apprehend Coke was not aware, related chiefly to the *delatores* or informers. The extension of the principle of these laws in England, by stat. West. 1. and 2 Rich. 2. relate to the spreading of *false* reports concerning persons in high station. To these succeeded the Statute de Scandal. Magnat.

These prosecutions for libel were principally brought in the Court of Star Chamber, a court consisting (as Lord Coke calls them) of the grandees of the realm, and acting without a jury. This court, organized by Henry 7th, and his son Henry 8th, behaved as a court so organized might be expected to behave, till the outcries of an insulted and indignant people caused it to be abolished in 16 ch. 1. Anno 1641. It was a great favorite of Lord Coke, who seems to exult, that it doth keep all England quiet.—4 Inst. 65. ch. 5. No wonder: its continuance constituted a reign of terror in that country. Mr. Holt, the compiler of the Law of Libel, seems to participate in Lord Coke's kind feelings toward that infamous tribunal; which, if we believe Mr. Holt, erred only in extending its jurisdiction too far; and not in its law: an opinion very grateful, I doubt not, to the legal palate of his patron, Lord Ellenborough. The general law of libel was not systematized or digested till the Star Chamber propositions, (for decisions they were not,) in the famous case, *de libellis famosis*, 3 James I. 1607, reported by Coke, Rep. pt. 5. p. 125, who appears to have brought on the causes, and drawn up the positions, (see Raynham's case, St. Trials, vii. p. 108.) so often referred to since his time. They are in substance as follows, viz.:

1. A libel may be made against a private person, or a man in public station, by writings, words, signs or pictures. In the first case, of a private person, it is punishable, because it incites to a breach of the peace: in the second case, it also brings scandal on government.

2. Although the person libelled be dead, it is punishable, as inciting to a breach of the peace. (The case before the court, was that of Lewis Pickering, who had written a ballad on a dead, and also on a living archbishop. The case *was not argued;* for the defendant confessed and submitted.)

3. A libeller shall be brought to trial by indictment, by bill, or in the Star Chamber; on his confession ore tenus.

He shall be punished by fine and imprisonment, by pillory and loss of his ears, as the case may require.

4. It is not material whether the libel be true or false, or the person libelled be of good or ill fame : for a party grieved ought to resort to the law, and not to libel.

Upon this judge-made law, not founded on any question or any argument then before the court, unsupported by any statute, or any previous decision, it may well be remarked, after Daines Barrington, (Ob. on the Stat. 94.) that the *only* question before the court could have been, the amount of punishment to be inflicted on a defendant who had submitted, and on whose offence there could have been no trial.

That the archbishop who complained, was not a magistrate: he attended the Star Chamber only, pro salute animæ.

That the prohibition of libelling a dead person, forbids all history of times past; for, as the court held, a government never dies.

That the truth cannot be given in evidence, in cases of libels, was then for the first time propounded. Even this proposition was denied in substance, by Powell and Halloway, in the case of the 7 Bishops; and it was in fact denied by Coke himself, in *Lake* v. *Hatton.*—Hobt. 253.

That a person may be guilty of libel, by signs or pictures, could not have been before the court, in a case of a song only.

The whole, therefore, is completely extrajudicial, and amounts strictly and literally to a code of laws drawn up by Coke, and enacted by the judges of the Star Chamber, on their own authority, not arising from the case before them, but with a view to cases that might arise. *And this is the foundation of the modern law of libel. I defy the lawyer who reads this, to show me any other.*

In 1633, Prynne wrote his Histriomastix, a philippic against stage plays and Sunday sports. In the accusation, it is stated, that their majesties sometimes were present at stage plays; and it was therefore a libel on them. Prynne was fined £10,000, branded in the forehead, condemned to perpetual imprisonment, slit in the nose, and had his ears cropped. The House of Commons to be sure, many years afterwards, declared the sentence illegal.—St. Trials, vol. 1. p. 418; Ib. 430. same year. Lord Balmerino, indicted for having mentioned, with all humility, that his majesty had put notes or marks against the names of certain persons who voted against the act relating to church government, "whilk is ane fearfu' "thing, for ane subject to pry into the gesture of his "sov'reign in his Supreme Court, and tending to di- "minish the glorious estimation and opinion of our "royal persons' equity and justice, in the hearts of our "subjects."—This libel was the humble petition of divers nobility and commissioners in parliament. Lord Balmerino was convicted, but pardoned. The court of Star Chamber was put down; but its spirit still ranged abroad like a roaring lion, seeking whom it might devour. In the trial of H. Carr, 1680, St. Trials, vol. 3. p. 57, Sir George Jefferies, the Recorder, states, that by the opinion of all the judges, it is the law of the land, that no one shall offer to expose to public knowledge, any thing that concerns the government, without the king's immediate leave. In the same year, however, (1680,) the House of Commons appointed a committee to examine into the decisions of the courts, in cases of libel: and the committee reported 12 or 14 cases tyrannical and illegal. The House reversed the decisions; and ordered *Scroggs*, *Jones*, and *Weston*, justices of the King's Bench; and North of the Common Pleas, to be impeached: and petitioned for the removal of Sir George Jefferies.—St. Tr. p. 217. 32 Ca. 2.

It was upon this occasion that Sir Francis Winnington observed to the House,—"the state of this poor nation is "to be deplored, that in almost all ages, the judges who "ought to be the preservers of the laws, have endeavored "to destroy them." At what period of the English history have they not been subservient to the views of the court ?*

3 St. Tr. 517.—In the trial of Thompson, Pain, and Farwell, (1682,) the Lord Chief Justice lays it down as law, that no private person has a right to find fault with the justice of the nation ; that is, with the proceedings in court.—See also 1 St. Trials, 333 ; 3 St. Trials, 505.

St. Trials, vol. 4. p. 304.—June 29th, 1688, came on the trial of the seven Bishops, for presenting an humble remonstrance to his majesty, against his gracious declaration for liberty of conscience. The judges were Sir R. Wright, chief justice, Halloway, Powel, and Allybone, justices :

* A lawyer of Philadelphia, William Rawle, Esq. has lately published a "View of the Constitution of the United States," in which I find the following compliment to judicial integrity, p. 273 : "*Party spirit never contaminates judicial functions.*" Every honest and well read lawyer will look aghast at the unblushing hardihood of this assertion. But this same Mr. Rawle was a prominent character among the ultra federal party, during the period emphatically called in Pennsylvania, the reign of terror. He was prosecuting attorney for the eastern district of Pennsylvania ; appointed under the administration of Mr. J. Adams ; and he was in that character, a coadjutor of his honor Judge Chase, of notorious memory : I make no complaint of his conduct on that occasion : but if Mr. Rawle's opinions were not duly estimated by the public, I might be tempted to say more on this subject. Perhaps Sir Francis Winnington may not be authority with Mr. Rawle : I therefore offer the following—General Alexander Hamilton, in the famous case of the People against Croswell, (3 Johnson's cases, 353.) is of opinion, "that the check on the press ought not to be committed to a "permanent bench of judges, who may be tempted to enter into the views "of government, and extend, by arbitrary construction, the law of libels. "How are our judges to withstand the combined force and spirit of the "other departments ? The judicial is less independent here than in England ; and of course, we have more reason and stronger necessity to "cling to the trial by jury, as our greatest safety. Men are not implicitly "to be trusted in elevated stations." See Lord Camden's letter to Almon ; and Mr. Erskine's description of the judicial bench in the times of Charles 1st and 2d, in his speech, in defence of the Dean of St. Asaph. Mr. Rawle may perhaps mean, that all existing judges are persons of pre-eminent wisdom and knowledge, of immaculate honor and integrity, perfectly free from all bias and prejudice, and unassailable, by any human interest or passions. Granted.

Sir Thomas Powis, Attorney-General; who states, that "these persons are not prosecuted as bishops, but as subjects, who censure his majesty's government, and give "their opinions on matters wholly relating to law and "government. * * * * No man may say of the great "men in the nation, much less of the great officers of the "kingdom, that they do act unreasonably or unjustly, or "the like: least of all, may any man say any such thing "of a king: for these matters *tend* to possess the people, "that the government is ill administered; and the consequence of that, is to set them on desiring a reformation." *The Chief Justice* told the jury, that the only question for them to consider was, whether the petition stated in the indictment, was the same with that delivered to the king. Whether it was a libel or not, was a question of law for the judges to determine. Judge Allybone said: "I think, in the first place, no man can take upon him "to write against the actual exercise of the government, "unless he have leave from the government, but he makes "a libel in what he writes, true or false. For if once we "come to impeach the government, by way of argument, "'tis the argument that makes it the government, or not "the government. So that I lay it down, that in the first "place, the government ought not to be impeached, by "argument, nor the exercise of it shaken by argument. "Then I lay it down for my next position, that no private "man can take upon himself to write concerning government at all: for what has any private man to do with "government, if his own interest be not stirred or shaken. "It is the business of government to manage matters relating to government, and of subjects to mind their "own. When I intrude myself into a man's business "that does not concern me, I am a libeller."

In this case, it was laid down by the Lord Chief Justice, that the words false and seditious, were inferences of law, and need not be proved. Powel and Halloway, however, seem to think otherwise. The Lord Chief Justice, in his charge, also stated, that whatever disturbs the government, or makes mischief and a stir among the people, is within the case de libellis famosis, and is a libel.

Hence it appears, that from the foundation case, introduced, organized, and digested by my Lord Coke, *de libellis famosis,* 5 Rep. 125. 1606, to the revolution of 1688, the constant struggle of the court, faithfully supported by the bench, was to blind the eyes of the public, as to the measures of government and the conduct of its officers: to deprive the people of all information out of parliament: to screen public delinquency of every description, at court and on the bench; and to establish the favorite position, that the people have nothing to do with the laws but to obey them.

Let us see whether the doctrines of the bench have been more palatable since the revolution in England of 1688, than they were before that time. St. Trials, v. 5. p. 527. Ann. 1704.—John Tutchin indicted for a libel, and convicted. The words were: " If we may judge by our " national miscarriages, perhaps no nation in Europe has " felt the influence of French gold more than England; " and it is worthy our greatest lamentation, that our dear " country should be thus weakened by men of mercenary " principles; when countries inferior to us in strength and " riches, are secured from attempts of this nature, only by " the fidelity of their people. What is the reason that " French gold has not affected Holland as well as England, " but that their ministry is such as is entirely in the interest " of their country, and altogether incorruptible. They " prefer men that are knowing in their posts and active in " business; while in England, we find out offices for men, " and not men for offices. By this, and by preferring men " by interest and favor, have the excise, the customs, and " other branches of the revenue, intolerably sunk; and by " this means has the navy of England, our great support, " been hitherto perfectly bewitched. And can Lewis " spend his money better, than in getting men into office "in England, who are either false or ignorant of business, "or who are his friends."

Lord Holt, Chief Justice, an honest man, but strongly imbued with the legal doctrines of the day, and devoted to his patron, King William, in summing up on Tutchin's case, observed to the jury: "To say that corrupt officers "are appointed to the administration of affairs, is certainly "a reflection on government. If persons should not be "called to account for possessing the people with an ill "opinion of the government, no government can subsist. "Nothing can be worse to any government, than to en-"deavor to procure animosities, as to the management of "it. This has alway been looked upon as a crime; and "no government can be safe unless it be punished. Now "you are to consider whether these words that I have read "to you, do not beget an ill opinion of the administration "of government."

Hence, whatever begets an ill opinion of the administration of government, whether truly or falsely, (for libel is ruled to be independent of truth or falsehood,) is libellous and punishable. Surely, where the press is open to both sides; where all the means of substantiating innocence, and disproving falsehood, are pre-eminently in the power of the government; where a simple denial of the *fact* would be sufficient to put the accuser on his proof before the public; where the parliament, also, are efficient to correct the errors of conduct in the government, and who will not stir without reasonable proof before them,—what harm can arise from an accusation before the public, which is liable to contradiction and refutation by the same privilege of the press that gave it birth? The sum and substance of this doctrine is, that no man shall be permitted (out of parliament) to publish any thing whatever, however well founded, that has the effect of accusing the measures of administration, whatever they may be, or of bringing them into public discussion; as much panegyric as you please, but no finding of fault. Whether this doctrine be calculated to serve the cause of the public, my reader must judge; more especially, as it has been repeatedly and lately determined, that a member of parliament has no privilege of repeating, out of the house, what he said in it, if it should contain any thing that a judge may deem libellous.—Rex v. Creevy, 1 Mawl. and Selwyn, 273. Mr. Creevy is a whig member, suspected of a tendency to radicalism; which will go far to explain this case, and reconcile it with the case of Horne Tooke.

St. Trials, v. 9. p. 273. 1729.—John Clarke was convicted of a libel for insinuating that the government was tyrannical, and the ministry corrupt.

St. Trials, v. 9. p. 255. 1731.—Richard Franklin indicted for suggesting that the ministry meant to break the treaty of Seville, and that a rumor to that purpose prevailed; fined £100.

In Easter term 1804, (Holt's Law of Libel, 125. 7 East. Rex v. Johnson,) William Cobbet was tried for a libel published in the weekly Register. Lord Ellenborough observed to the jury: "It is no new doctrine, that if a "publication be calculated to alienate the affections of the "people, *by bringing the government into disesteem;* "whether by ridicule or by obloquy, the person so con-"ducting himself, is exposed to the inflictions of the law. "It is a crime: and has ever been considered so: whether "wrapt in one form or another. The case of the King v. "Tutchin, has removed all ambiguity from the question." This doctrine was the ground of decision, in the cases of Holt, Winterbottom, Eaton, Wakefield, Simmons, and Jordan. See also 1 Hawk. ch. 73. sect. 7. and the cases collected in the notes to the American edition of Holt on Libel, 117. 125. Hence, the recent, the present law of England, propagated, detailed, approved, by writers and compilers even in this country, is, that any thing may be published in favor of government, of the measures of government; of the conduct and characters of ministers of government; whether the panegyric be a disgraceful specimen of base and time serving adulation or not: but that no person is justified in publishing any thing of an opposite character, however well intended, to open the eyes of the people; however well founded in truth and in fact, or however important to be known.

Is this a doctrine calculated to promote the public interest? Is this a doctrine that a free people ought, for their own sakes, to support? Is this a doctrine calculated to do credit to the bench or the bar of the United States? Is this republican doctrine?

But may not a jury judge for themselves, whether a publication of a political nature be true or false—well or ill intentioned—useless or mischievous? By judge-made common law, no. By the common law of common sense, yes: for there can be no crime in publishing facts or observations useful to be known; true in themselves; and made known with a good intention toward the public: although persons in power may be exposed, evil deeds brought to light, and bad characters developed. The more checks the people can reserve to themselves, on the conduct of persons in power, the better for the people; for the attempts to encroach on intrusted authority are unwearied and never ceasing: the more avenues there are to political truth, the more extensively, the more accurately will it be known. In the name of common sense, what reasonable motive can be assigned for prohibiting, denouncing, and punishing useful information? Governors and judges, indeed, may revolt at it; but the people, the people, what motive can *they* have to shut their eyes and ears, and decide in the dark? Moreover, by the common law, that law which has existed before any assignable period of legal recollection, the *intention* of the person who commits an act said to be criminal, is of the very essence of the crime. To say that a jury can judge of a fact brought before them, and shut out all evidence and consideration of the motive and intention involved in it, is a gross absurdity, and contrary to analogy of every other criminal accusation. The intention, the quo animo, constitutes the crime; but the modern doctrine, the judge-made law of libel, calls upon the jury to declare upon their oaths, that a man is *guilty* of publishing the truth with an honest view of giving useful information. Nay, if libel or no libel be inference of law to be made by the judges, the jury are bound on their oaths to say that a man is *guilty* of that which the court, a few days afterwards, may consider as innocent. For as the fact of publication alone is before the jury, and as the verdict guilty applies to that alone, the court may take their own time to consider whether the publication be praiseworthy, innocent, or guilty. So, the court, after verdict of guilty, may be moved in arrest of judgment; inasmuch as the guilty publication pronounced guilty by the jury, is not a libel in law. To what then can the verdict of guilty, apply? Unless to the mere naked fact of publication uncoupled with intention; and totally devoid of innocence or guilt. To such dreadful nonsense and disgraceful quibbling, have the judges been driven, from their own anxiety, lest the jury should open their eyes to their own rights, and take common sense into their consideration, when they pass a verdict! However, let us see how the law formerly stood, and how it stands now, as to the admission of the truth to be given in evidence on indictment for libel. I have already stated some of the objections to that most impudent batch of propositions laid down as law by Lord Coke, in his Star Chamber case de libellis famosis,—a case in which there was, and could have been no debate and no decision. The defendant came into court and submitted on terms; and the only question was the quantum of punishment. There was and could have been no other.

The law of England consists of *statute law*, commencing with magna charta, and the statutes of Westminster; and *common law*, in use before that period; and probably founded on positive enaction, whose origin and existence cannot now be traced, owing to length of time that hath intervened. I deny that there are any other sources of the law of England. I challenge any other to be found in any book of legal authority or character. The binding force of the common law, is not derived from long usage, any further than that long usage amounts to prima facie evidence that it had been originally enacted by competent authority, and therefore obeyed.

The case of Lewis Pickering, or de libellis famosis, 5 Co. Rep. 125. took place in the Court of Star Chamber, 3 Jac. 1. An. 1606, soon after Breverton's case, 2 Jac. 1. I ask of any lawyer who may read these pages, whether the common law dates its origin from the reign of James I. and the time of Lord Coke? Can any proposition be legally taken as part and parcel of the common law, which was never known, or stated, or practised as law, before that time? Now I aver, that there is no authority to be found for prohibiting a jury to hear the truth on matter of libel, before the reign of James I. If it be asserted as law before the case of Lewis Pickering, show me the ancient book wherein it is to be found. The act of Scand. Mag. gives a qui tam action: and it is held that truth cannot there be given in evidence, *because the king is concerned as plaintiff on the record.* Moreover, whence did the Court of Star Chamber, who decided without the intervention of a jury, derive their right of deciding the law of jury trial? Or whence does any court derive their authority, not merely for deciding a point of law, but for enacting a code of law, not included in the case before them, not argued and debated, and not judicially considered after argument? Do we, in the present day, give the weight of conclusive authority to obiter dicta, nisi prius decisions, or volunteered declarations in dubious cases? The case de libellis famosis was an impudent fraud on the public: and Lord Coke deserves the execrations of posterity for the part he took in this legal forgery. It is in this way the people of England have been cheated and bullied out of their rights by tyrannical judges, the tools of a court; and time-serving lawyers, the slaves of the bench.

In the case of Lake v. Hatton, Hob. 253. Coke himself stated that the truth might be given in evidence. If the Countess of Exeter (said he) had a purpose to poison, Hatton might have justified; which, says Hobart, I denied: for a libel, though true, cannot be justified.

On a review of the charges of the judges, in the case of the seven bishops, it appears that the Chief Justice, and Justice Allybone, were of opinion, that the jury had no right to pass upon any point in the case, but the mere fact of publication. The other two judges, Powel and Halloway, deemed the intention of the person accused, and the words "false, scandalous, seditious," material, and to be judged of by the jury. The jury did so.

In the case of Penn and Mead, indicted for libel in 1670, the Recorder told the jury they had only to find whether the defendants preached or not: for, whether the matter and intention of their preaching was libellous or not, were questions of law, and not of fact; which fact they were to keep to, at their peril. The jury brought in a verdict of acquittal; and the court fined them forty marks each. Bushel, one of them, refusing to pay this fine, was committed; and on habeas corpus, Lord Chief Justice Vaughan decided the commitment to be illegal; acknowledging the right of the jury to pass upon the whole matter. Vaughan's Rep. 135.

In the trial of Thompson, Pain, and Farwell, 1682, St. Trials, 505. for libel, Chief Justice Pemberton left it to the jury to decide on the whole evidence, whether defendants were guilty or not, of the offence of "*affronting* "*the public justice of the nation, with a design to make* "*people believe there was no popish plot.*" Ib. 517. Verdict, guilty.

So in the case of Tutchin, (5 St. Trials, 527. Anno 1704,) Holt left it to the jury to find whether the words cited did not beget an ill opinion of the administration of the government. Coke's Star Chamber law, therefore, was enforced gradually, and not without exception and hesitation.

Fuller's case, tried before Holt, (5 St. Trials, 442. 444; 8 St. Trials, 78; 3 Johns. Cases, 387.) was, on information, for publishing two false, scandalous, and defamatory libels. It was not as McNally says (on Evid. Vol. 2. p. 649.) on the Statute of Scand. Mag. for the information does not conclude *contra forman statuti;* it was therefore at common law. Nor was Fuller prosecuted merely as a cheat and impostor, but as a false and malicious libeller. The Chief Justice addressed him in these words: "*Can* "*you make it appear that these books are true? If you* "*take on you to write such things as you are charged* "*with, it lies upon you to prove them at your peril.* "*These persons are scandalized, if you produce no proof* "*of what you charge them with. If you can offer any* "*matter to prove the truth of what you have written, let* "*us hear it. If you have any witnesses, produce them.*"

If this does not clearly show, that by the common law, in cases of prosecution for libel, according to Lord Chief Justice Holt's opinion, a defendant had a right to offer the truth in evidence; then words have no meaning. Yet the Court of King's Bench, a few years ago, in the case of the King v. Burks, 7 Durn and East, 4. decided that *falsely* was not necessary in an indictment for libel; and that the truth cannot be given in evidence, as the indictments against Eades, Tremaine, 61; against Tutchin, 5 St. Trials, 527; against Franklin, 9 St. Trials, 255. did not contain that allegation. So that the doctrine of Buller, in Rex v. Dean of St. Asaph, 3 Durn and East, 42. continued and continues the law of this day in England, Mr. Fox's bill notwithstanding; which, however, has thus far been of use, that though the judges do now, in all cases, instruct the jury that the question, libel or no libel, does not belong to the jury to decide; yet if the jury think fit to decide it, their verdict is not impeachable on that ground. Holt's practice did not conform to the modern doctrine. In the case of Peter Zenger, indicted for a libel at New-York, August 4th, 1735, 9 St. Trials, 275. the jury brought in a general verdict of acquittal ; agreeing with the defendant's counsel, (Mr. Hamilton,) that the words false, scandalous, and malicious, were material, and ought to be proved. The court were of a contrary opinion.

In the case of Owen, charged with having published a libel on the House of Commons, in the matter of Alexander Murray, 11 St. Trials, Append. 197. the jury, against the charge of the judge, who declared the question of libel or not libel, a question of law merely, brought in a verdict of not guilty: notwithstanding, therefore, Breverton's case, 2 Jac. 1. and the case de libellis famosis, 3 Jac. 1. there was no settled and authoritative decision that took away from a jury the right of deciding on all the points connected and involved in an indictment for libel, until the King v. Clerk, 1729, Bernard. K. B. 304. for publishing Mist's Journal. In this case, Lord Raymond informed the jury, that the fact of printing and publishing only was in issue. He was followed by Lord Chief Justice Lee ; who was followed by Lord Chief Justice Ryder ; who was followed by Lord Chief Justice Mansfield ; who was followed by Lord Chief Justice Kenyon ; who was followed by Lord Chief Justice Ellenborough ; and by all the herd of judges, without exception, at the present day : and that in spite, and in the very teeth of Mr. Fox's libel bill, 32 Geo. 3. ch. 60. which does not enact as new matter, but declares that mere proof of publication by the defendant, and of the sense ascribed to the words of the supposed libel, shall not be sufficient of themselves to ground a verdict against the defendant ; but that the jury may give a general verdict of guilty or not guilty upon the whole matter put in issue. Now, the points put in issue are, *the fact of publication, the application of the innuendoes, the truth or falsehood of the supposed libel, and the intention of the writer or publisher.* That act declares proof of the two first points to be insufficient; of course it lets in the others. If the publication be false, malicious, or seditious, punish it: but what punishment should be inflicted for a publication well intended, honest, just, and true? The act allows the judge to give his opinion and direction to the jury on the matter in issue, between the king and the defendant. Under this clause, the judges have uniformly given it as their opinion, in the teeth of the act, that libel or no libel is a question of law for the court, and not for the jury to decide. This was done by Ellenborough, Abbot, Best, Bailey, Holroyd, in the cases of Sir Francis Burdett and others, 4 Barn. and Ald. 95. and by the Recorder at the Old Bailey, Newman, Knowlys, in the case of John Clarke, 1824. Thus has the plain meaning of Mr. Fox's libel bill been quibbled away; and the act itself rendered a perfect dead letter, so far as the bench can influence the jury. Such is the libel law of England as it now stands, in cases where what is called the government, or any of the persons administering it, are accused of misconduct. The enlightened state of public opinion, of late years, in that country, has kept the conduct of the ministers and judges under some control: but the law, as it is, and as it may be enforced, without departure from legal authority, is quite strong enough to suppress all political discussion, to punish the most useful truths, and to prostrate the liberties of the people. Whenever the ministry feel themselves strong enough, they may as safely count on the Bench of Judges, as on the Bench of Bishops. Mr. Pitt, the worst minister that Great Britain ever saw, in *all* respects, went near to effect this purpose. Another minister of the same stamp, may effect hereafter what he left undone. Deeply tinged as our own judges too commonly are, with the spirit of English law, and with reverence for English decisions, every point relating to the state of the law and the state of public opinion, in that country, on the question of libel, becomes of intense importance here; but I hope our judges begin to feel their own superiority, and they will do well to act upon it.

The result of this investigation into the state of the English law, on political libel, is as follows.

The whole system is calculated to screen the government of the nation, the ministers, the public officers of every description, as much as possible, from public investigation, by making every charge of misconduct brought against them, libellous and punishable as a crime, and suppressing, as far as possible, all inquiry by the press.

For this purpose, the judges, who from the earliest period to the present day, have played into the hands of the government and the persons in power, have of their own accord, created a system of judge-made law, not founded on any statute law, and not to be found in any part of the common law, previous to the time of Lord Coke. The whole question may be seen well stated on both sides, in the case of the People against Croswell, in 3 Johnson's Cases, 337; nor is it to be found so well stated any where else.

Under pretence of declaring what the common law is, the judges of England have in innumerable instances, more particularly in the case of libel, enacted laws suited to their own views and purposes, and to the views and purposes of those who govern. So that three-fourths of what is now considered as indubitable law in that country, is neither statute law, nor common law, but law made by the judges, and no where to be found but in decisions reported from the beginning of Elizabeth to the present day; receiving additions and alterations, as new cases, new questions, and new circumstances of society have arisen, heretofore unforeseen and unprovided for; alterable, altering, fluctuating, and uncertain, from the different capacities, tempers, and designs of the judges who enact and change it at pleasure. The law of libel, in particular, has been in a continued state of doubt and uncertainty from the Star Chamber case of Lewis Pickering, in Coke's Reports, to the present time; but almost always decided with a leaning toward the interests and inclinations of "the pow-

"ers that be." So that it is utterly false to assert that the law of England is either statute law or common law: the greater part of it is neither.

That the right of the jury to judge of the intent of the party accused of libel, and to receive evidence of the truth of the facts charged as libellous, so as to rebut the presumption of malice, though supported by Powel in the case of the seven Bishops, by Chief Justice Vaughan, in Bushel's case; by Holt, in Fuller's case, (St. Tr. vol. 5. p. 441;) by Lord Camden, in Wilke's case, 2 Wils. 150; by Lord Loughborough, in the House of Lords; by Lord Erskine, repeatedly, in deliberate publications, has been resisted, and fought, inch by inch, by the courts, till the juries have been completely conquered and deprived of this right; and compelled to pronounce that conduct to be guilty, whose intent and meaning they are forbidden to inquire into; and which the judges claimed the exclusive right of pronouncing guilty or innocent, after the return of the record of conviction, (the postea.) Under this doctrine, if a man be indicted for publishing the Lord's prayer, the jury must bring in a verdict of guilty; and the defendant is driven to a motion in arrest of judgment, six months afterward, inasmuch as the Lord's prayer is not a libel! In this manner the crime of libel is made a perfect anomaly in the criminal law; and the jury are deprived of that privilege which belongs to them in every other criminal case, of considering the intention of the supposed offender. An anomoly, however, absolutely necessary to the protection of political delinquency.

That notwithstanding Mr. Fox's bill (32 Geo. 3.) was passed to restore the juries to their lost right of deciding the whole case in question of libel, the Judges have contrived to explain away that act of parliament, and set it at nought. At this day they openly charge the juries, that with the truth or falsehood of what is published,—with the good or ill intention of the publisher, or tendency of the publication,—with all that really constitutes criminality, they have nothing to do; this being matter of law exclusively for the court, and the court only to decide. So stands the law of England. Common sense, however, and common justice requires the rule laid down by Lord Camden, to be adopted. "In truth, the crown, in a libel, should not "only prove the words to be false, but likewise show, "either from the nature of the paper itself, or from exter-"nal proof, that it was malicious as well as false: or I "would acquit the defendant."—Letter to Almon, p. 14.

In these United States, the law of libel may be considered as commencing with the passing of the sedition law, 14th July, 1798. This law permitted the truth to be given in evidence by the defendant; but as the constitution of the United States had prohibited congress from *passing any law whatever*, abridging *the freedom* of speech or of the press, it was so clearly and indisputably unconstitutional, that nothing could account for this usurpation of prohibited authority but the rancor of party politicians, who felt that they had power, and forgot that they *wanted* right. Several convictions took place under this law, while Judge Chase sat as a judge of the federal court; and before him. The objections to the constitutionality of the law, were decided in its favor. The law, however, became so obnoxious to the people, that it was the main cause, if not the chief, of Mr. J. Adams losing his re-election as President. But as the law expired by its own limitation, without having been repealed, the decisions in favor of its constitutionality and its provisions, have rendered it doubtful whether the principles of that law may not hereafter be considered as the actual law of the land, so far as the jurisdiction of the federal courts extends.

The privilege conceded by that law, of giving the truth in evidence, was absolutely nugatory, considering the infinite trouble, the enormous expense, and the time requisite to procure evidence of the plainest propositions. For instance, I was convicted under that law for having stated, inter alia, that Mr. Timothy Pickering, the Secretary of

State, had, with the consent of the President, written to Judge Bee, of South Carolina, a letter relating to the giving up of Jonathan Robbins, claimed as a British deserter, but alleging himself to be a citizen of the United States, born at Danbury in Connecticut. I stated this to be an improper interference of the executive magistrate, with the exercise of judicial authority. The fact was notorious, generally asserted, never denied, and no where disbelieved. The court however might have required me to *prove*, by evidence technically legal, that Judge Bee was a federal judge of South Carolina; that Timothy Pickering was Secretary of State; that such a letter, and for such a purpose, was written and transmitted to Judge Bee, a district judge of South Carolina, by Timothy Pickering; and with the knowledge and consent of the President Adams, (who, the court decided, could not be cited or compelled to attend as a witness.) The proof of these facts, in a manner strictly legal, would have been attended with an expense, a labor, and a vexation, equal of themselves, to no slight punishment. Then again, the jury were selected by the marshal, a man of known and opposite political feelings, who, however otherwise respectable he might have been, was the creature of the President, appointed by the President, removable by the President, and biassed to have a defendant in such a case convicted. This most objectionable mode of selecting juries still prevails. We borrowed it, like all our bad legal customs, from the British practice. Much to the honor of the present ministry, Mr. Secretary Peel's bill of last session, has altered all that; and a defendant in that country, may now stand a chance of being tried by a fair and unbiassed jury. Can we say this here? No.

Although the facts stated in the alleged libel were matters of notorious and universal belief, and the conclusions such, as a large majority of the nation, (who afterwards expelled Mr. J. Adams from the presidency, at the close of his first term,) were perfectly satisfied about. Yet I never heard a doubt expressed before the trial, among my own friends, and those who thought politically as I did, of my conviction. It was considered to be a measure fixed and determined on: and I took little pains about the trial, firmly persuaded that no trouble I could take, would be of any avail. Such was the rancorous character of political party at the time, that I believe all the persons concerned in, and contributing to my condemnation, Judge Chase and a very few others excepted, were misled into a conscientious conviction, that they were doing right. It was a period when politics, both foreign and domestic, were of a character uncommonly interesting and exciting. Nor do I feel that I have personally more reason to complain of the virulent injustice of one party, more than its opponents. I shall by and by make practical use of the preceding remarks.

The case of the People v. Croswell, 3 Johnson's Cases, 337. came on, in the Supreme Court of New-York State, on Feb. 13th, 1804. It was an indictment against a printer for a libel on Thomas Jefferson, then President of the United States. The Chief Justice who tried the cause, charged the jury, among other things, that the question of libel or no libel was a question of law, a legal inference from the facts; that if the jury were satisfied that the defendant published the piece charged in the indictment, and that the innuendoes of the indictment were true, they ought to find the defendant guilty; that the intent of the publisher, and whether the publication in question was libellous or not, was, upon the return of the *postea*, to be decided exclusively by the court; and therefore it was not his duty to give any opinion to the jury on those points; and he gave none. He read to the jury the opinion of Lord Mansfield, in the case of the Dean of St. Asaph, 3 Term Rep. 428. and said that was the law of the state of New-York. Verdict, guilty.

Motion for a new trial: 1. Because the judge had refused to put off the trial, to give the defendant time to procure testimony to *prove the truth of* the libel. 2. Because he had mis-directed the jury in stating, that the question of libel or no libel, was a question of law exclusively for the court to decide, and not for the jury. The points are admirably well argued in favor of the defendants, by Hamilton, Harrison, and Van Ness; and by the Attorney-General (Spencer) and Caines, for the prosecution. There is no case of libel embracing the above questions, to be found in the English reports, so well argued on either side, as the case in question. The court were equally divided in opinion; and the motion for a new trial was therefore lost; but the reported case contains the opinions delivered from the bench by *Kent*, Justice, in favor of giving the truth in evidence; and in favor of the right of the jury to pass upon the question of libel or no libel; and the opinion of *Lewis*, Chief Justice, against these positions. Those who wish to show, that by the law of England, prior to the case de libellis famosis, the truth of the facts could not be given in evidence, in an indictment for libel, will do well to fortify themselves by perusing Chief Justice Lewis's arguments and authorities; which, in my opinion, are far from proving the point he wishes to establish; but insufficient as they are, better arguments and authorities are not to be found. I do not examine them here, because the whole case is so well worth attention, that no man can be competent to decide upon the questions thus put at legal issue, without carefully perusing it.

General Hamilton advanced as law, the following doctrine of libel, which was adopted in the same words by Judge Kent; and which has my full concurrence.

" *The liberty of the press consists in the right to pub-*
" *lish with impunity, truth, with good motives, and*
" *for justifiable ends; whether it respects government,*
" *magistracy, or individuals.*"

Such was the impression made on the public, by the arguments of General Hamilton and Judge Kent, that at the next session of the legislature, an act (*not enactive but declaratory*) was passed by an unanimous vote, on the 6th of April, 1805. The preamble is, " Whereas doubts have

" arisen whether on the trial of an indictment or information for a libel, the jury have a right to give their verdict " on the whole matter in issue." Then the first section declares, that they shall have a right to determine the law and the fact, under the direction of the court, in like manner as in other criminal cases: and shall not be required by the court to find the defendant guilty merely on proof of publication by the defendant, and of the sense ascribed to the publication in the indictment. The defendant shall have a right to move in arrest of judgment, as heretofore.

Section second provides, that the defendant shall be at liberty to give in evidence, the truth of the matter contained in the alleged libel; which shall not be of itself a justification, unless it also appear that the matter charged as libellous, was published with good motives, and for justifiable ends.

Sect. 3, limits the punishment to 18 months imprisonment, and 500 dollars fine.

Sect. 4, takes away all prosecution for libel by information.

Something is still wanting beyond these provisions to furnish a perfect security for the freedom of the press. 1st. Under the present mode of selecting juries in the federal court, no defendant can be assured of a fair and impartial trial. 2dly. The right of the defendant to require a prosecutor to be endorsed on the indictment, should be given to him at least a month or six weeks before trial. 3d. The prosecutor should be required a month previous to the trial, or on the filing of the indictment, to deny upon oath, the truth of such facts as are stated as true in the libel, and which he means to controvert as being false. A defendant should not be put to strict proof of facts, notorious or commonly believed, or that cannot honestly be contradicted. He ought to be bound to prove every material fact denied upon oath, and no other. In England, a prosecutor applying to the Attorney-General for a criminal information for libel, is, I believe generally, if not always, called upon previously to deny upon oath, the truth of the facts charged in the libel. (Starkie on Libel, and Doug. Rep. Rex. v. Haswell, 372.) 4th. The law of New-York appears to embrace only cases of libel against the government, persons in office, and individuals: it does not clearly extend to the clerical division of libels. On this last class, the New-York decision, in the case of the People v. Ruggles, exhibits, I must be permitted to say, for reasons that I shall adduce, no very creditable specimen, either of sound law or sound sense; notwithstanding the well merited reputation of Judge Kent, who delivered the opinion from the bench. In August term of the same year, 1805, the court was again applied to for a new trial, in the case of Croswell, which was unanimously agreed to by the bench. I believe the prosecution dropt, and was no further proceeded in.

This case of the People against Croswell, was not reported by Mr. Johnson, till 1812, otherwise it would probably have had an influence on the Court of Appeals in South Carolina, in the case of the State v. Lehre, January term, 1811. It had already been decided in Massachusetts, in Respub. v. Clap, 4 Mass. Term Rep. 163. 1808, that the truth might be given in evidence to negative the charge of malice and an intent to defame; but the mere truth of the facts was not of itself sufficient to justify the libel. The defendant must show in addition, a justifiable intent. It was also decided on that occasion, that where a man becomes a candidate for a public office, he puts his character in issue, so far as respects his qualifications and fitness for the office; and the publication of the truth on this subject, with an honest intent of informing the people, is no libel. But the publication of calumny and falsehood against public officers and candidates, tends to mislead the public in their choice, and is a gross offence, properly punishable by indictment. Chief Justice Parsons decided the course to be thus: first, show that the publication was well intentioned; then, that is true.

The liberty of giving the truth in evidence, on an indictment for libel, was supported, also, in the Municipal Court at Boston, Massachusetts, in December term, 1822, at the trial of the Commonwealth v. Joseph T. Buckingham, for printing and publishing a libel on John N. Maffit. I copy part of the opinion of the court as to the liberty of the press, and the rights of juries in cases of libel. The part that precedes it, relates to a question that had been raised on that trial, whether the prosecuting attorney could consent that the truth of the libel should be given in evidence. The court decided, that if it could not be given in evidence, under the existing constitution and law of Massachusetts, the prosecuting attorney could not make it evidence by consent. The court (Honorable Josiah Quincy, Judge,) proceeds thus :—

The court inquired of the attorney for the county,—if the law of Massachusetts denied the right to a defendant to give the truth in evidence in these cases, where he obtained the power to give that right?

The attorney replied, that he deduced it from the general power of parties to waive, by a mutual agreement, any particular advantage the law gave to either.

The court replied, that it had considered this subject with great care and anxiety, and it was satisfied, that if the law of Massachusetts was, as the counsel for the government stated, the court had no right to permit such an agreement. This case was not like the common one of inadmissibility of evidence, arising out of the want of form, or the existing of interest, or out of the mere nature and relations of evidence itself. The ground upon which, by the English common law, the truth was denied to be given in evidence, in case of libel, was, because the truth or falsehood of the allegations was no constituent part of the crime. In other words, it is as much a libel if it be true, as if it be false; that is, it is as much a crime.

If the doctrine asserted be law, what then is the effect of admitting the truth in evidence? If it is to have any effect, the effect must be *to make that no crime, which previous to such concession was a crime.* Can the concession of the attorney alter the nature of the thing? The language of such a course of proceeding would be, "true or false, this publication is a crime: but the attorney says, that if the defendant can prove the truth, it shall be no crime: yet the law says, that although it be true, it is a crime." Now can concession of counsel make that no crime, which is a crime? Besides it is admitting a power to exist in the hands of the counsel of the government, with which, in the apprehension of this court, the law intrusts no individual: for it is nothing less than the power, at will, of making an act a crime, or no crime. He can make "fish of one, and flesh of another," at his election.

If, therefore, it be true, as is asserted, that, by the law of Massachusetts, the truth shall not be given in evidence, in cases of libel, this court has no doubt concerning its duty. In such case, it can have no question that it has no right to admit such evidence by agreement.

The court, therefore, deems itself reluctantly compelled to examine the doctrine of law, which is asserted by the counsel for the government.

The question concerning the admissibility of the truth in evidence, in case of libel, has, on two recent indictments, been brought under the consideration of this court. In one case, the libel was against the *holders of public elective offices*: in the other, against *the public agent of a public elective officer.* Both came within the principle of the doctrine laid down by Chief Justice Parsons, in the case of Commonwealth v. Clap, 4 Mass. Rep. 163. Both, also, were so undeniably within the principle of the liberties secured by our constitution, that this court could have no hesitation concerning its duty to adopt the doctrine of that case as applicable to those cases, without farther investigation.

The same question is now raised in a case differing materially in character, from both of the preceding. The libel charged in the present indictment, is neither against the holder of a public elective office, nor against a candidate for such office, nor against any agent of such holder. In the present case, the libel charged is against an individual, who, whatever may be his connexion with a particular religious society, stands in relation to this question, on the same ground as every private citizen. And the question now to be considered is, the admissibility of the truth in evidence in the case of libels, occurring in the use of the press, against a private citizen.

The case of the Commonwealth v. Clap, has no conclusive bearing on the question, arising under the present indictment. That was a case of a public posting of another for "a liar" and a "scoundrel." It did not occur, in the use of the liberty of the press. Neither the counsel for the government, nor those for the defendant, in their respective arguments, nor the court in giving its opinion in that case, alluded to any such liberty. It had, apparently, no connexion with the question then before the court. That which is now under consideration, is strictly and necessarily a question concerning the nature and extent of the liberty which the press, under our constitution, enjoys. In other words, the question now to be considered is, whether the right to give the truth in evidence, in all cases of public prosecution for publications occurring in the use of the press, does not necessarily result from the terms of the Constitution of Massachusetts.

Considered in relation to this constitution, the question stated is a question of alleged repugnancy between a particular liberty secured by that constitution, and a particular doctrine existing at common law.

The particular liberty is the liberty of the press, which the constitution declares to be "essential to the security of freedom" in a state, and that "it ought not therefore to be restrained in this commonwealth." The particular doctrine of the common law is, "that in public prosecutions for libel, the truth of the facts alleged in the publication, shall not be given in evidence."

The alleged repugnancy, is between the principles of this doctrine and the nature of that liberty.

The first question that now arises is, whether there be any such repugnancy?

If there be none, then there is an end of the whole inquiry. The liberty of the press is safe, and the principles of the doctrine are to be maintained.

If there be any such repugnancy, then the resulting question is,—which is paramount, the particular liberty or the particular doctrine? In other words, if both cannot exist together, which must yield;—which shall be limited, the nature of the liberty by the principles of the doctrine, or the principles of the doctrine by the nature of the liberty?

Although this last question is in its nature subsequent to the other, yet, as I apprehend, there can be no division of sentiment upon it, among lawyers, it will be useful now to state its nature and relations.

The 6th section of the 6th chapter of the Constitution of Massachusetts is, that clause under which the colonial and all antecedently existing laws derive their force and authority. And that clause contains an exception which abrogates "such parts of those laws as are repugnant to the rights and liberties contained in this constitution."

This is as express a constitutional declaration as can be uttered, that in all cases of such repugnancy, the exception is to be made out of the principles of the doctrine of the antecedently existing law; and not out of the nature of the constitutional liberty.

The only question therefore is, whether there be any repugnancy between the nature of the liberty of the press, and the principles of the common law doctrine. If such repugnancy exist, there can be no question that, under our constitution, the principles of that doctrine must be limited by the nature of the liberty.

Before entering upon the general question, it seems proper to state a rule of construction, applicable to all cases, *arising under the constitution of this nature*, which appears to this court to be as clear and unquestionable as any conclusion of reason can be.

In all questions touching repugnancy between a particular liberty, existing under the constitution; and a particular doctrine existing under the antecedent law, the essential constituent character of that liberty, is to be sought in its own nature; and not to be sought in the principles of the doctrine alleged to be repugnant. For it would be absurd to take the principles of a particular doctrine as the limitation of the nature of a particular liberty, when the question in controversy is, whether the nature of that liberty does not necessarily limit those very principles?

What the nature of the liberty of the press is under our constitution, must be sought, therefore, in its own nature, and not in the principles of the antecedent law. The doctrine of libel is, in all countries, a doctrine of power. In England the object has been to draw questions of this class from the jurisdiction of the jury to that of the court. The means by which it has been effected, are the assumption by the court of three principles.

1st. That criminality in publications depends upon their general tendency, and not upon the publisher's particular intention.

2d. That the tendency of the publication is a question of law, to be decided by the court, and not by the jury.

3d. As the general tendency of a publication may be to public mischief, notwithstanding the facts alleged in it be true, that it follows in such cases, that the truth or falsity of those facts is indifferent; and that therefore the truth shall not be allowed to be given in evidence.

In the course of this argument it will be attempted to be shown, that the first of these principles is false in nature; the second, false in fact; and the third, false in consequence.

The question, however, first to be considered is,—

What is the liberty of the press?

When we have found what that is, we have attained that which the constitution declares (part 1. art. 16.) is "essential to the security of freedom in a state";—and which "ought not therefore, to be restrained in this commonwealth."

"The liberty of the press," whatever it is, courts of justice have no right to restrain.

The great question then is, what is that liberty?

It is not becoming a court of justice to deal in popular declamations and flourishes concerning the liberty of the press.

Its business is to analyze every subject; and among the depths and mysteries of its nature, to detect those fundamental principles which, because they inhere in it, and are inseparable from it, constitute its law.

The question here raised concerning the liberty of the press, has nothing to do with public opinion, or popular excitement; it is a naked abstract inquiry, instituted for the purpose of satisfying ourselves concerning our duties.

What then is the liberty of the press?

First. What is the press?

It is an instrument,—an instrument of great moral and intellectual efficacy.

The liberty of the press, therefore, is nothing more than the liberty of a moral and intellectual being, (that is of a moral agent,) to use that particular instrument.

The question, therefore, concerning what is the liberty of the press, resolves itself into two inquiries.

1. What is the liberty of a moral agent to use any instrument?

2. Is there any thing in the nature of the instrument called the press, which makes the liberty of a moral agent to use it, different from his liberty to use any other instrument?

As to the first inquiry, there can be but one opinion. As a general rule, the liberty of a moral agent to use any instrument, depends upon the motive and end he has in using it.

For a good motive and a justifiable end, he has a right to use it; that is, he has a liberty to use it.

For a bad motive and an unjustifiable end, he has no right to use it; that is, he has no such liberty; in other words, such use of it is licentiousness.

Liberty is, in relation to every other instrument, characterized by, and coextensive with, the nature of its justifiable use. And this depends upon the quality of the motive and of the end.

If A thrust B through with a sword, and he dies, A has used an instrument over which he had power; whether in that, he was guilty of an act of licentiousness, for which he is obnoxious to punishment, or merely exercised an authorized liberty, for which he shall go free, depends not upon the fact, or the effect, but upon the motive and end which induced the thrust.

If A be indicted for the murder of B, A's guilt or innocence depends, not upon the conclusion of law to be declared by the court, resulting from the fact of the blow given, and the effect of death which followed; but it depends upon the conclusion, concerning the intent or motive of the moral agent to be declared by the jury.

If A should be indicted for the murder of B, and the counsel for the commonwealth should contend, and the court should decide, that the jury had nothing to do with the intent or motive, which was the occasion of the thrust; but that their sole province was to decide, 1. the fact that A made the thrust; 2. the effect that B died by it; and that the intent, motive, and preconceived malice, was a conclusion of law from that fact and that effect, to be declared exclusively by the court. A doctrine so repugnant to common sense, would not be endured one moment. Yet this is the precise doctrine of the English courts of common law, in the case of libel. It is that doctrine on which depends, and solely depends, the other doctrine, that the truth shall not be given in evidence by defendants in public prosecutions for libel.

For if the liberty to use the press depended, like the liberty to use every other instrument, upon the quality of the motive and the end; and if the jury, in deciding the guilt or innocence of the accused, had a right in these prosecutions, to take into consideration the intent, motive, or end, as they have in deciding guilt or innocence in every other prosecution,—then the right to give the truth in evidence, would follow necessarily and of course. For the truth or falsity of the allegation is, in all such cases, an inseparable quality of the intent or motive, and whatever jurisdiction has the power of deciding concerning the intent or motive, must of necessary consequence, have the power of considering and deciding upon such truth and falsity, whether the object of the defence be to justify the act, or to excuse the malice.

It follows, that by denying to juries the right to decide on the intent or motive, in making the publication, and by this only, have the English courts of law deprived the defendant of the right of giving the truth in evidence.

It also follows, that if, by the principles of our constitution, juries have the right to consider the intent or motive, in deciding every question concerning guilt or innocence,—then that, the right of giving the truth in evidence, is a necessary consequence.

Now this right of deciding upon the intent or motive, is inherent in juries, in every case of public prosecution, except in the case of libel. Why this exception?

If A uses the press to assail the reputation of B, he makes a thrust at the reputation of B, by the use of that weapon called the press. If A make a thrust at B, with the weapon called a sword, in case of a public prosecution for that act, he has the right to show the intent or motive with which he gave the thrust.—Why shall he be denied the same right, when he makes a thrust at him with the weapon called the press?

This brings us to the second and great inquiry in this case.

Is there any thing in the nature of the instrument called the press, which makes the liberty of a moral agent to use it, different from his liberty to use any other instrument?

The liberty of a moral agent, in the use of every other instrument is, as has been shown, coextensive with good motive and justifiable end. The question therefore resolves itself into this:

Is there any thing in the nature of the instrument called the press, which makes the liberty of a moral agent to use it, not coextensive with a good motive and justifiable end?

In other words,—Is it possible, that in a free country, under a constitution which declares the liberty of the press is essential to the security of freedom, and that it ought not to be restrained,—is it possible that it is not the right of every citizen to use the press for a good motive and justifiable end?

If this be, as I think, incontrovertible: if, necessarily, every citizen has such a right; then if called in question for such exercise of right, has he not also, consequently, a right to prove the goodness of the motive, and the justifiableness of the end? Can the law or constitution give a right to use an instrument for a particular purpose, or under a specific modification, and deny the right of proving that it was used for that purpose, or under that specific modification?

If, then, he have a right to prove the motive and end, must he not have a right also to prove it, according to its nature? That is to say, if, from its nature, the proof to be adduced be a matter of fact, can it be doubted that he has a right to prove it as a matter of fact, before that jurisdiction which, under our constitution, has the only cognizance of matter of fact—the jury?

Can it be questioned that motive, end, intent, are in their nature matters of fact?

Are they any thing else than qualities of the act of a moral agent? And if the act of such agent be a fact, can the qualities which inhere in it, and are constituent parts of its nature, be any thing else than facts?

If facts,—are they not cognizable by a jury, and subject of proof like other facts?

In the opinion of this court, this right is as inherent in every citizen under our constitution; and a court of justice have no more right to deny to a person charged with a malicious use of the press, the liberty to show that its use was, in the particular case, for a good motive and a justifiable end, than it has a right to deny to a man indicted for murder, the liberty to show that he gave the blow for a purpose which the law justifies.

Both these liberties lie within the same reason, and are founded on that fundamental and universal law of moral nature, according to which, guilt or innocence in a moral agent, is solely qualified by motive or intent.

If this reasoning be just, the liberty to use the press is, like the liberty to use any other instrument, coextensive with a good motive and justifiable end.

The right so to use this instrument, necessarily includes the right to show such motive and such end, if prosecuted for it. And this includes the right of giving the truth of the facts alleged in evidence, as inseparable in the nature of things, from the goodness of the motive and the justifiableness of the end. For such a motive and end, falsehood can never be published. It follows necessarily, that to prove the truth of the fact, is essential to the very existence and nature of such a defence.

It is in vain to say that the principles of the common law deny to a man indicted for a libel occurring in the use of the press, the right to show his intent, motive, or end. For if, as has now been attempted to be demonstrated, the right to show the intent, motive, or end of the act done, in the use of the liberty of the press, is included in, and inseparable from its very nature, then the denial of this right, by the principles of the common law, is repugnant to that liberty, and as such is abrogated by the terms of our constitution. The great reason on which English courts declare the common law excludes the truth in these cases, is, that the law punishes publications of a libellous character, on account of their *public* mischief; that is, of their tendency to produce breaches of the peace. Publications have this tendency, it is said, as well when they are true, as when they are false: therefore, truth, in such cases, makes no difference. Now these general consequences attending the unrestrained liberty of the press, were as well understood at the time of the adoption of the constitution, as they are at this day. The restraint upon the liberty of the press, effected by this principle, had been for years, even in England, the subject of complaint, clamor, and denial. Why did the framers of our constitution adopt, in relation to the liberty of the press, a breadth of expression, which necessarily includes the right of always using it for good motives and justifiable ends, if it was their intention that any citizen so using it, should be made in any case, criminally responsible, without the possibility of producing his intent for his justification? If it had been their intention that the liberty of the press should be limited, by the principles of the common law, would they have used expressions which necessarily limited those principles, from their repugnancy to that liberty?

Touching the three principles, by the assumption of which English courts of common law have, as has been stated, effected the withdrawing from the jury the jurisdiction of intent and tendency in cases of libel, and on that raised the doctrine of the inadmissibility, in such cases, of the truth in evidence;—The first is, that criminality in publications, depends upon their general tendency, and not upon the publisher's particular intention. Now this, in the apprehension of this court, is false in nature.

In the nature of things, the only foundation of criminality, in a moral agent, is—intention; by which is meant, will—to do either a particular *mischief*, or some *general* mischief.

If any act of a moral agent be of such a nature as to have, at one and the same time, a particular tendency and a general tendency, the law, often and justly, considers such act a crime; because of the mischievous nature of its general tendency, although the particular tendency may have been innocent.

Thus, if A ride a horse accustomed to strike with his heels into a crowd and a man be killed by him, it may be murder or manslaughter in A, according to the circumstances. A crime of some kind it will be. Why? Because, although the particular intention of A might have been innocent, yet he having been guilty of an act of general mischievous tendency, and the only evidence, in such case, of his general intent being the nature and general tendency of the act; the law, which is only elevated reason, admits, and justly, the general mischievous tendency of the act, as evidence of a general mischievous intent. But here, as in nature, criminality consists in the intent. Tendency is the evidence of that intent.

But this doctrine would not answer the purpose of English courts of justice; because intent being a fact, the jurisdiction of the question, as a fact, would be transferred to the jury; which it was the purpose of the court to keep in their own hands. Therefore nature was contradicted. Criminality was made to depend upon the tendency of the act, instead of the intent. It was now only necessary to make the tendency of the act a question of law, and the magic circle was completed; the jury excluded from the cognizance of the question; and the whole power vested in the court.

Accordingly, this is the second principle adopted by English courts of justice. That the tendency of the publication is a question of law; and of consequence, to be decided by the court, and not by the jury. Now this, also, is false, in point of fact.

Tendency, in the nature of things, is a fact, whether it be physical or moral. What is tendency? It is direction of an act to an end. If A aim, with an axe, a stroke at a tree, and he kill B, the direction of the blow is a fact, upon which a jury will have to decide, when considering the guilt or innocence of A.

So in morals, if a man be indicted for blasphemy, the tendency and meaning of the words are a question for the jury, as matter of fact.

The same is true of general tendency, as of particular tendency.

Tendency, by being general or particular, is only altered in circumstance not in nature.

If A throw down from a scaffolding, carelessly, into a crowded street, a piece of timber upon B, and he die; it is a crime in A, in consequence of the general tendency of the act. Can any one doubt that the circumstances on which the general tendency depends, (that is, whether a street or not,—or frequented or not,—or with precaution or not,) are not facts to be considered by a jury?

Why is not the general tendency of a publication also a fact?

The particular tendency of the terms is a fact: for courts permit juries, even in England, to decide upon the applicability of the innuendoes. If particular meaning be a fact, why is not general meaning a fact? In the nature of things there is no ground for the doctrine, that the general tendency of publications, is not a matter of fact. As such it belongs exclusively to the jury. And of all facts, it is the last of which a jury in this country, should be divested.

A constitution, which grants to the citizen the liberty of the press, secures to him also, from the very nature of that grant, the liberty of using language according to its common meaning and ordinary acceptation. If called into question for the use of that liberty, he has a right to have the meaning, acceptation, general tendency, or bearing of the words, decided by that tribunal, which, by our constitution, is the exclusive judge of fact, and who will decide upon that meaning, tendency, bearing, or acceptation, according to their general nature or effect; judging by the use of common life and common sense, and not according to artificial skill, or any technical refinement. For which reason, among others, in the opinion of this court, the third doctrine of the English courts, that the truth shall not be given in evidence in cases of prosecutions for libels, is false in consequence. For if the jury have a right to decide the intent and tendency, the right to have evidence of the truth, follows necessarily and of course. It is not to be denied, that there are evils inseparable from the abuse of the liberty of the press, as from the abuse of every other liberty. But it is secured by our constitution, in terms, as this court apprehends, expressly devised, and certainly having the effect, to abrogate the asserted doctrine of the English common law, in this commonwealth. The true language of the Constitution of Massachusetts is this: It is better for the public to take the risk of the evils, and for individuals to suffer the inconvenience resulting from a press without other restraints, than those which are consequent on the obligations of good motive and justifiable end, than for the state to incur the dangers resulting from any uncertainty in the tenure of a liberty, which, as it declares, is " essential to the security of its freedom."

It would be easy to extend this argument into one of a general and popular tendency; but sufficient, as is apprehended, has been urged to support the doctrine, that intent and motive is as much an inquiry for the jury in these, as in any other indictments; and that of consequence, the right to give the truth in evidence, in all cases of public prosecutions for libel, occurring in the use of the press, is the necessary result of the terms in which the liberty of the press is secured by the Constitution of Massachusetts.

The court has confined itself to a strict and single deduction of the right in question, from the essential nature of the liberty of the press. Not that the question did not admit of being maintained by an argument drawn from precedents and authorities, arising under the English common law. But it is impossible for this court to add any thing to the deep, learned, and conclusive arguments of Judge, now Chancellor Kent of the State of New-York, and of the late Alexander Hamilton. Both of them among the greatest men and lawyers of the age. Their arguments, stated at large, (in 3 Johnson's Cases, p. 337.) are as complete as they are unanswerable. The doctrine here maintained is deduced by them from the ancient fountains of the common law, as they existed in its early purity. The modern doctrine of libels being, in the course of their analysis, satisfactorily proved to be "an usurpation on the rights of the jury," not justified by the fundamental principles of the common law. To adopt the language of Chancellor Kent, "*The true rule of law is, that the intent and tendency of the publication is, in every instance, to be the substantial inquiry on the trial, and that the truth is admissible in evidence to explain that intent, and not in every instance to justify it.*" The comprehensive and accurate definition of one of the counsel at the bar, (Alexander Hamilton,) is perfectly correct. "That the liberty of the press consists in the right to publish, with impunity, *truths with good motives and for justifiable ends*, whether it respects government, magistracy, or individuals.—3 Johnson's Cases, 394.

I proceed now to examine the doctrine laid down in the State of South Carolina v. Lehre, decided in the Court of Appeals at Charleston, by the unanimous opinion of all the judges. The opinion of the court was delivered by Judge Waties. I make no apology for the freedom I use with this opinion. My friend Judge Waties will require none. What motive, indeed, can old men, like ourselves, cherish, but that of leaving behind us our testimony in favor of *truth*, wherever it may be found ?

The counsel appear to have argued thus :

Prior to the case de libellis famosis, all the laws relating to libel and offences against government, were made expressly for the punishment of *false* tales ; and therefore do not include *true* tales : they imply, therefore, that under those laws, the truth might be given in evidence.—Stat. West. 2 Rich. 2 ; 1 and 2 Phil. and Mary.

To this the judge replies, that although this be as it is

stated, it does not follow that because particular acts were passed on special occasions, that the common law did not punish true tales published for a malicious purpose. I grant this does not follow. There is no evidence whatever on either side. But if the judge says the common law *did* so punish true tales, let him show it. I deny that he can. The rule of law is, *affirmantis est probare:* and the judge will recollect the old law maxim to the same purpose, *de non apparentibus et non existentibus eadem est ratio.* That is, we must apply the same conclusion to things that do not exist, and to things of whose existence there is no evidence.

But, says the judge, we need not explore the dark recesses of ancient law; it is enough that all the great expounders of the law, from Lord Coke down to Mr. Justice Blackstone, have uniformly laid it down as a rule of the common law, that the truth of a libel cannot be given in evidence in a criminal proceeding.

To this I reply, that they have not uniformly laid down this rule. Instances of repeated exception, I have already given. Mr. Fox's *declaratory* bill was enacted to take away doubt whether the jury could pass upon the whole matter of libel put in issue, which of course includes the truth or falsehood of the libel, and the intent of publication. But suppose the bench decisions were uniform from Lord Coke downward; I should be glad to know what right the court of Star Chamber, which first enacted it, had to enact Sir Edward Coke's positions into a law, without one single precedent in the books to support it; and in despite of common sense? It is easy to account for it, from influence of the court, and the time-serving spirit of Coke himself and the judges, but in no other way. Either this decision is common law, or it is not. If it be, show it before the time of Lord Coke; if you cannot show it, if you have no proof whatever of its being common law, it is the forged and fabricated common law of the bench, and not of the country. Can any one who has read the history of the times, doubt for a moment, about the obsequiousness of the judges, in the times of James I. and Charles I.? About their readiness to declare that to be law, which the court wished to be so?

The judge says, Mr. Fox's act allows the jury to decide on the criminality of a libel, so far as the libel itself is evidence of it. Where does the judge find this in Mr. Fox's act? I cannot find any thing like it. I can find in it that the jurors may give a general verdict on the *whole* matter; and that they shall not be required to find the defendant guilty, merely on proof of publishing and on the sense ascribed to the libel in the indictment or information. Now, does not the *whole matter* include the question, whether the defendant published what was true, with a good intent; or what was false, with a malicious intent? I well know that the judges of England, from the Star Chamber cases to the present time, have sedulously moulded, so far as they dared, the doctrine of libel to suit the views of the court: but we have no inducement here to follow in the same path.

The judge says, we are not to look for the common law among its first sources, and ancient decisions; but we are to collect it purified by modern decisions, which have made it conformable to reason. So that the common law is a mere nose of wax, to be moulded as modern judges think fit. I know it. But this is the first time it has been avowed from the bench, that the common law is whatever judges, by way of improvement, choose to make it. The bench, therefore, contains the most efficient legislators of the country: and judge-made law and common law are synonymous. I grant that the judges have, in many cases, greatly improved upon the common law. I grant that one undoubted principle of ancient common law, may be the legitimate parent, under new and unforeseen circumstances of many decisions that are just in themselves, and that could not have been contemplated two or three centuries ago. That such decisions have been unavoidable and beneficial. But under this unlimited license, the judges have, in a thousand instances, become legislators. They have brought forward and enacted, not the law, which has necessarily branched out as the legitimate offspring of ancient principles, but law heretofore unknown—spick and span new. The judges are, in fact, the legislators of the country; and until the representatives of the people shall resume their rights, and assume their duties, by ordering a code or digest to be compiled for the purpose of enacting it, they will and they must be so; acting in good faith, and with upright intentions. But under the modern doctrine, as laid down by Judge Waties, may they not alter and mould the law as they please? It is an awful power they have (perhaps unavoidably) assumed; and the public are hardly aware of the extent to which it may be carried. In the case of libel in England, I cannot doubt of their bias toward the wishes of government: all I hope is, that the judge-made law of that country, decided under that notorious bias, may not be followed implicitly here. It is the duty of juries to prevent it.

But Judge Waties proceeds to say, that the right of giving the truth in evidence, in cases of libel, was denied by the Roman law; and he cites a passage to this purpose, from the Pandects. The words he cites, are the words of Domat; but not a syllable to that purpose is to be found in the Pandects. Nothing is a part of the Roman civil law, but what is contained in the Corpus Juris Civilis. The passage in question, I believe, is not to be found there. But the direct contrary doctrine is expressly laid down in the Pandects—Lib. 47. tit. 10. ch. 18. *Eum qui nocentem in framavit non esse bonum equum ob eam rem condemnari: peccata enim nocentium nota esse et oportere et expedire.* This is laid down by Paulus: General Alexander Hamilton also cited Perezius on the code, vol. 2. p. 208; and Vinnius on the Institute, 762. Lib. 4. tit. 4. I have examined that part of the Pandects which should contain it, (De Injuria et de libellis famosis,) but there is no authority for this passage cited by Judge Waties from Domat, who gives none himself. I am aware that Holt (on libels, p. 29.) says, there is no doubt that the civil law forbade the truth to be given in evidence. But he cites no authority but Spanish and German commentators. Show me the authority, where alone it can be found, in the Corpus Juris Civilis. The judge's authority from Justinian's Institutes, L. 4. tit. 4. contains nothing like it. Nor does his reference to Domat, V. 3. tit. 12. The Emperor Ch. 5. and M. Bayle, are no authorities in our courts for what the law is. His citations, therefore, are all mistakes. It is most probable then, (says the judge,) that the rule is derived from the civil law. Now the civil law does not authorize this rule, but directly the reverse. "*It is right and proper, says the civil law,* "*that the offences of the guilty should be made known,* "*and he who publishes them, ought not to be punished* "*for so doing.*" The judge states, that it appears by Croswell's case in New-York, that it was the law there, that the truth could not be given in evidence. He was mistaken: on that point, the court were divided: but finally, they were unanimous, *that it could.*

As to the modern authorities cited by the judge, Lord Coke and Sir William Blackstone, they are nothing to the purpose. Can the judge show me any statute law for his opinion, previous to Coke's case? Can he show me any common law authority for it, previous to that case? No: the law then may be Star Chamber law; Coke's law; government law; bench-enacted law; but it is not the law of England, according to any known or recognized authority, unless the judges have a right to substitute themselves for the parliament. That they often do so, I allow. Have they a right to do so? That is the question.

The People v. Croswell had been decided, but I suspect not reported till after Lehre's case; otherwise I am persuaded Judge Waties would have entertained more doubts on the subject than he did when he delivered the opinion of the court.

In fact, I suspect the judge was misled, by not distinguishing between cases where the libel consists in the malice, and not in the falsehood of the publication. Suppose one man heedlessly publishes of another that he is deranged, or that he is impotent, and makes him an object of ridicule, on account of this misfortune: can the truth be a justification in such a case as this? But suppose the prosecutor were about to contract marriage with a relation of the defendant; would not the truth of the imputation be of the very essence of the case? This is strongly supported by Rex v. Harvey, 1823, 2 Barn. and Croswell, 257.—Justice Bailey's opinion. The truth can never be given in evidence but for the purpose of explaining the intent of the publication, and negativing the charge of malice. But when malice is manifest upon the face of the libel itself, *granting it to be true*, the truth can be no justification. All this is so well put by Judge Waties, p. 818, 819. that I am tempted to transcribe the passage, from South Carolina v. Lehre.

"These reasons for not allowing the truth of a libel to "be given in evidence in a criminal proceeding, are fully "sufficient to justify the rule. But there is another rea-"son for it, which will be thought by many to give more "value to it than any other. It serves to protect from "public exposure secret infirmities of mind and body, "and even crimes, which have been repented of and for-"given. Who will say that the truth of these should be "given in evidence to satisfy or excuse the exposure of "them? A man may have been overcome by some "strong temptation, and been induced to commit a crime "which he has since abhorred; for which, by a long per-"severance in virtue and honesty, he made his peace with "all who could be injured by it; and has thus a well "grounded hope of obtaining pardon from his God. A

" woman, too, who may have yielded to some seducer, or " been the willing servant of vice, may have since become " the faithful partner of some worthy man, and the mo- " ther of a virtuous offspring ; her frailties have long been " forgiven, and she is in the enjoyment of the esteem and " respect of all her neighbors. Will any one say that " these expiated sins may be dragged from the privacy in " which they have been sheltered ; that they may be pre- " sented to the view of an unfeeling world ; be punished " by disgrace and odium, in which innocent connexions " must participate ; and that the author of all this misery " may justify the act by showing the truth of the charges ? " Shall he be allowed to disturb the sacred work of re- " formation, and rob the poor penitent of the blessed fruits " of her repentance ? Justice, charity, and morality, all " forbid it, and, thank God ! the law forbids it also."

All this, well said and truly said as it is, has nothing to do with political libel ; when to tell the truth is beneficial to the public, and to tell a falsehood is to mislead them. The judge's opinion, therefore, is well confirmed by Vinnius, in the passage quoted by Kent, in the People v. Croswell, 3 Johns. Cases, 378,—" This principle in the law of " libels, is considered as rational and sound in an ethical " point of view, by Paley, Mor. Phil. p. 188 ; and to this " extent, the writers on the civil law have allowed the " truth to excuse a defamatory accusation. The opinion " of Vinnius, in his commentaries on the Institutes, Lib. " 4. tit. 4. § 1. is so pertinent and forcible, and he states " the just distinction with such perspicuity, that what he " says merits our particular attention. *Three things* " *are usually questioned here. First, whether the truth* " *of the libel amount to a justification. The general* " *opinion of commentators is, that it does, in cases* " *where the public are interested to know the truth. As* " *if a man be accused of being a thief, a murderer, an* " *adulterer, &c. Under this head comes the answer of* " *the lawyer,* (*in L. cum qui* 18 *in pr. hoc tit.*) *where he* "*says, that he who libels a guilty man, ought not to be condemned for so doing. For it is expedient that the crimes of the guilty should be made known. So, if this supposed defamation should take place before a magistrate, for there all is presumed to be so managed, that every thing proper to be known, should be given in evidence, on an investigation that takes place as to the crime alleged. But it is otherwise, when a desire of doing an injury is reasonably collected from the circumstances; as if the libellers should be tempted through hatred to do this, during an impending quarrel: in such case, malice ought not to go unpunished.* —L. 3. C. d. off. rec. prov. *But if the accusation made against the complainant, is of such a nature that no one is interested in being informed of it, as if an offender has already suffered the punishment of his offence, or if any natural infirmity be imputed; as if he said of any one, he is club-footed, or one-eyed, or hunch-backed; the truth of such a charge is no justification; for it is fairly presumed to arise from malice. The person so libelled, however, is at liberty to disprove the charge.*" (Judge Kent cites the original which I have here translated.)

I would add the following case. One man is indicted for asserting of another that he has the itch; thereby occasioning him to be excluded from society. The truth has nothing to do with the matter, say the judges. Yet if the accusation be true, it was the duty of the defendant to make it: if untrue, it is a falsehood properly punishable. So of the small-pox.

I object to the judge's opinion, therefore, not its limited application, but its sweeping generality. I make no objection to it as applied to the eloquent passage I have quoted. But, suppose I say of a man, he offered a bribe to a member of the legislature to procure the passage of a bill, in which the person I am accusing was interested: he indicts me for libel. Is it possible for the words "guilty or not guilty" to be pronounced by the jury, if they are prohibited from hearing evidence, whether the fact be true or false? If it be true, the public ought to thank me for telling it. I do it at my peril. Has not the prosecutor a full remedy against me, if the charge be false, by an action of slander, in which the truth or falsehood of the charge can be met, and wherein the damages will be proportioned to the injury? Why am I to be put to the trouble and expense of indicting him, when the ends of the public are fully answered by the course I have taken? Compelling a man to become a prosecutor, at the hazard of his character, the loss of his time, his trouble, and his money, is a sure way to screen the guilty. If the fact I assert be not true, he can compel me to the proof by a civil action. An indictment often amounts to strong evidence of the guilt of the prosecutor.

Sir Francis Burdett writes a letter in Leicestershire, exclaiming in the natural terms of honest indignation, against the detestable outrage committed on the unoffending populace at Manchester. An Englishman who would speak of it in terms less indignant, ought to be driven from society, as a disgrace to his country. He was indicted and convicted, *because the alleged libel charged a triable offence.*—4 Barn. and Ald. 95. So that, before an honest man in Leicestershire can give his opinion of an open, public, undenied, and undeniable outrage in Manchester, he must quit his family, journey to the spot, leave all his own business afloat, however pressing, and occupy himself, for a twelvemonth, in searching out the offenders, procuring evidence of their guilt, superintending the whole course of law proceedings, fee counsel, attend the trial, hear the verdict of the jury, and the judgment of the court, and *then,* but not before, in the improbable case of a conviction against persons protected by government, he may venture to say, the action they were guilty of was an offence. Why in the name of common sense and common honesty, is this the law upon which society should proceed? Are the judges authorized to put this gag into the mouth of every man in the country, and in solemn mockery to call it a free country? Yet is this the law here; if the State v. Lehre be law. Most assuredly this is not the way to render the citizens attached to the laws; and as it is an indictable offence, "to affront the law," who is a very touchy and waspish old lady, many a man may incur the hazard of getting his face scratched, who cannot fall in love with these decisions.

In the State v. John Allen, (McCord's So. Car. Rep. 525. May, 1822,) Judge Johnson stated, that the intent of the publication complained of, was matter of law for the court to decide on: and that if the jury found a general verdict, it would amount to no more than finding the fact of publication and the truth of the innuendoes. General verdict of guilty. Motion for a new trial, on the ground of misdirection in point of law. Judge Huger delivered the opinion of the court above. He did not seem to deny that the libellous character of the publication was matter for the court, and not for the jury; but the case of the State v. Lehre had decided that a general verdict embraced the *whole case;* and not merely the fact of publication, and the sense ascribed to the words of the libel. New trial granted. There is, therefore, in this our state, a manifest leaning toward the restrictions on the press, which the judges of the parent country have thought fit to impose.

It would be in vain for me to deny, if I were so inclined, the great good sense, the patient attention, the laborious investigation, the considerate decision of the English bench. As a general position, and in common cases of meum and tuum, it has my full concurrence and approbation. But from the very commencement of judicial history in that country to the present hour, the judges have, in fact, been under a strong bias to support the measures of government, right or wrong. They tread the beaten path of those who have gone before them: and all the modern notions of the rights of the people, and the rights of the press, that have taken so strong hold on public opinion, they regard as criminal innovation; because they find the contrary doctrines laid down as law, in the pedant pages of Lord Coke and his cotemporaries. Because their predecessors have been the servile tools of the court, they think they must be so too. The law in England is a very ignorant profession. In this country, every lawyer considers that he may be called upon to act as a legislator: his line of reading and reflection, therefore, branches out; and he puts himself in the way of all the liberal opinions which the extent of modern investigation have brought into public view. If he does not, he ought so to do. Not so in England; where the profession of the law, confining a man to the beaten mill path of his predecessors—making it the rule of his opinion *stare decisis*, never to wander from precedent, however absurd—making it the rule of his practice to estimate truth and falsehood, in proportion only as they are profitable—and to practise the law, not as an enlightened and liberal philosopher, but as a shoemaker makes shoes, or a stonecutter polishes his marble,—in that country, I say, the profession is a profession of narrow-minded and selfish practitioners, who are universally regarded when in parliament, as the hired advocates of the ministry, on the one side; or the opposition, on the other; and out of their proper element, when they assume to be legislators. Two or three honorable exceptions are not sufficient to alter the truth of this general position. In this country, our judges are not inferior to the occupants of the British bench, in patient research, in temperate decision, or in the talent of discovering legal truth. They have also the incalculable advantage of practising in a country, where the liberality and freedom of our political institutions, give a masculine tone and character to public opinion, that act most beneficially on the profession of the law generally. Why should they suffer themselves to be shut up like children in the go-cart of British precedent? It is time they should universally feel and act upon their own superiority, and occupy the vantage ground, which the spirit of our free government affords them. I have endeavored in these pages to show the illiberal, time-serving character of the British law of libel, a system, out of harmony with all our republican institutions; and which, therefore, neither ought to be, nor can be, the law here. The legislatures of New-York and Louisiana, and the bench of Massachusetts, have long been of this opinion, and have acted on it. I hope it will be acted on, in like manner, throughout these United States. The following propositions by General Alexander Hamilton, in the People v. Croswell, 3 John. Ca. 360. on the freedom of the press, I hope will ere long be universally considered among us as well settled law. It is high time they should be so.

1. The liberty of the press consists in the right to publish with impunity, truth, with good motives, for justifiable ends, though reflecting on government, magistracy, or individuals.

2. The allowance of this right, is essential to the preservation of a free government; the disallowance of it, fatal.

3. Its abuse is to be guarded against, by subjecting the exercise of it to the animadversion and control of the tribunals of justice: but this control cannot safely be entrusted to a permanent body of magistracy; and requires the effectual co-operation of court and jury.

4. To confine the jury to the mere question of publication, and the application of terms, without the right of inquiry into the intent or tendency—reserving to the court the exclusive right of pronouncing upon the construction, tendency, and intent of the alleged libel,—is calculated to render nugatory the function of the jury; enabling the court to make a libel of any writing whatsoever, the most innocent or commendable.

5. It is the general rule of criminal law, that the intent

constitutes the crime: and it is equally a general rule, that the intent, mind, or quo animo, is an inference of fact to be drawn by the jury.

6. If there be exceptions to this rule, they are confined to cases, in which not only the principal fact, but its circumstances, can be, and are specifically defined by judicial precedent, or by statute.

7. That in respect of libel, there is no such specific and precise definition of facts and circumstances to be found. Consequently, it is difficult, if not impossible, to pronounce that any writing is per se, and, exclusive of all circumstances, libellous. Its libellous character must depend on intent and tendency: the one and the other, being matter of fact.

8. The definitions or descriptions of libels to be met with in the books, found them upon some malicious or mischievous intent or tendency to expose individuals to hatred or contempt, or to occasion a disturbance or breach of the peace.

9. That in determining the character of a libel, the truth or falsehood is in the nature of things, a material ingredient; though the truth may be not always decisive: but being abused, may still admit of a malicious and mischievous intent, which may constitute a libel.

10. In the *Roman law*, one source of the doctrine of libel, the truth in cases interesting to the public, was given in evidence. The ancient statutes probably declaratory of the common law, make falsehood an ingredient of the crime. The ancient precedents in the courts of justice, correspond. The precedents to this day, charge a malicious intent.

11. The doctrine of excluding the truth as immaterial, originated in a tyrannical and polluted source, in the court of *Star Chamber:* and though it prevailed a considerable length of time, yet there are leading precedents down to the Revolution, and ever since, in which a contrary practice prevailed.

12. This doctrine being against reason and natural justice, and contrary to the original principles of the common law enforced by statutory provisions, the precedents that support it deserve to be considered in no better light than as a *malus usus*, which ought to be abolished.

13. In the general distribution of power, in any system of jurisprudence, the cognizance of *law* belongs to the court; of *fact*, to the jury. When they are not blended, the power of the court is absolute and exclusive. In civil cases, it is always so; and may rightfully be so exerted. In criminal cases, the law and the fact being always blended, the jury, for reasons of a political and peculiar nature, for the security of life and liberty, are entrusted with the power of deciding both law and fact.

14. This distinction results—1. From the ancient forms of pleading in civil cases, none but special pleas being allowed in matters of law; in *criminal*, none but the general issue. 2. From the liability of the jury to *attaint* in civil cases; and the general power of the court in granting new trials as its substitute; and from the exemption of the jury from attaint in criminal cases; and the defect of power in the court to control their verdicts, by new trials: the test of every legal power being its capacity to produce a definitive effect liable neither to punishment nor control.

15. That in criminal cases, nevertheless, the court are the constitutional advisers of the jury in matters of law, although the jury may compromit their consciences, by lightly or rashly disregarding that advice. But the jury may still compromit their consciences, by following the advice of the court; if exercising their judgments with discretion and honesty, they have a clear conviction that the charge of the court is wrong.

So far General Hamilton, whose propositions are fully substantiated by Judge Kent and himself. That all this is sound law, fully sanctioned by legal authority, as these able men have shown, I have no doubt; and I think I also have shown it, in the foregoing pages. But I should be inclined to add to these legal propositions, the following additional safe-guards, which my experience of the practice has suggested. I would enact the foregoing propositions in a declaratory law entitled "an act for securing the freedom of the press; and declaratory of the law of libel;" adding to it the following clauses.

16. In all cases of prosecution for libel, the court may instruct or advise the jury; but shall have no authority to require or direct them what verdict they shall bring in; the whole matter in issue, with all the circumstances of truth or falsehood, intent, motive, and design, being within the right of the jury to decide upon, after hearing all the evidence, and the charge of the court.

17. A defendant in a prosecution for libel, shall have a right to call for a prosecutor to be endorsed on the indictment, at least one calendar month previous to the trial.

18. In order that a defendant may not be put to needless trouble, expense, vexation, and delay, the prosecutor shall be required, and it shall be his duty, one calendar month before the trial, to deny upon oath the truth of such assertions as are charged to be false and libellous; and the truth whereof he requires the defendant to prove upon the trial. And the defendant shall not be called upon or expected to be prepared with proof of the truth of any part of the matter charged as libellous, except that part which shall have been so denied upon oath. This may be required in England. (See Starkie on Libel, 601. and the cases there cited.)

19. On the trial, it shall be competent for the defendant, in proof of the facts charged to be libellous, to offer in evidence, public notoriety or public rumor: and the jury shall decide whether the public rumor or notoriety so offered in evidence, be or be not reasonably sufficient to justify the defendant in stating the facts complained of; to the extent and in the manner in which they are stated in the publication alleged to be libellous.

20. And whereas political society is instituted for the

purpose of regulating the conduct of men towards each other, while they live and continue members of the same political community; and not for the purpose of regulating opinions which relate to another state of existence; and when all political rights and obligations are dissolved by death: therefore—

No person shall be liable to punishment for examining, affirming, or denying the truth of any religion, or any tenet of religion, or for advancing any opinion relating to religion, or investigating any subject of controversy of any kind, on account of its connexion with or bearing upon any tenet or doctrine of any religion whatever: provided, such investigation shall be conducted in a manner not offensive to public decency, and with an honest design of discovering the truth; of which design the jury shall judge according to the circumstances of the case that may be made out before them. It being the undoubted right of every man to publish for the information of his fellow citizens, on any and every subject, any opinion whatever that he may deem true, and interesting to them to be informed of; provided this be done with honesty and good faith, for the purpose of communicating what he may deem useful information; of which intention the jury as aforesaid, shall judge from the facts of the case.

21. In all cases of libel, either party may require to be tried before a special jury, on the usual notice established by the rules of court: which special jury shall be selected from forty-eight jurors, chosen by ballot out of the whole number of citizens liable to serve on juries at that court, by the returning officer, in the presence of the defendant or his attorney, at a reasonable time, and with reasonable notice previous to the commencement of the term. The special jury to be struck from the list of the forty-eight jurors aforesaid, in the usual manner, by or on behalf of each party to the prosecution.

I now proceed to the ECCLESIASTICAL part of my subject, the law relating to that class of libels which are termed heresies and blasphemies.

I have gone through the division of heresy against the prevailing politics of the government; and I come now to heresy against the religion of the priesthood.

Quarrels about religion were very rare, during the times of Paganism. They began among the Apostles, not long after our Lord's ascension. Disputes arose between Paul and Peter, about the obligation of conforming to the ceremonies of the Mosaic law; and James's epistle is manifestly written to counteract the opinions of Paul, on the exclusive efficacy of faith. Afterwards, these disputes increased among the early Christians, till the time of Constantine, 325 years after Christ, when Christianity became for the first time, a religion exclusively by law established. Hitherto, the numerous disputes in the Christian church, had been chiefly confined to literary warfare; and I speak of it with great regret, to mutual forgeries and falsehoods, and had not involved the government in any of the unintelligible points of controversy that were engendered in those days, from presumptuous ignorance; controversies which, in lieu of real knowledge, begat only envy, hatred, malice, and all uncharitableness.

When Constantine had established as the true faith, the creed of his own adherents, the power of the government was incessantly employed in exterminating all variation and opposition: and thus it has continued, with more or less vigor, to the present day. Men (as Jortin says) have been compelled not to think alike; for that is impossible: but to say they do. When persuasion and command were equally unavailing, resort was had to those holy means of conversion, the sword, the fire and the faggot, prison, confiscation, and the pillory: and these have been employed without mercy. The religious exterminators have acted wherever they dared to exercise power, as Galgacus complained the Romans acted *ubi solitudinem faciunt, pacem appellant.* "They convert an inhabited region into a wilderness, and they call it peace." Fear made hypocrites of infidels; and the propagandists exulted in their success: it was with them a manifest conversion to the true religion, by the most orthodox and persuasive of all arguments. And thus it has continued throughout the Christian and the Mahomedan world to the present times; with the sole exception of this country; where the spirit of persecution, by law, is nearly extinguished. It exists more in public opinion, among those who are well meaning but ill informed, than in the letter of the law; but still too much, both in the one and the other. Increased knowledge and free discussion will gradually set every thing on its proper basis. Our laws, our modes of thinking, our habits, our literature, are all drawn from Great Britain. The remnant of intolerance that still remains among us, is supported partly by the influence of the law of that country, on the subject of religion; and partly by the strong aid afforded to it, by the interests of the clergy; who subsist by propagating the opinion, that of all crimes, heresy and infidelity are the most dreadful, because they appear more than any other to threaten a curtailment of clerical influence. Profoundly ignorant of the philosophy of the human intellect, they consider infidelity as a voluntary crime. Let us then examine the conduct of the church establishment in our parent country; and the progress and present state of the law which has been at various times enacted to support that establishment. I do not want to notice the outrageous positions taken, during the tyrannical *reign* of Henry 8th. Elizabeth appears on the 29th of December, in the 26th year of her reign, first to have given, as head of the church, *exclusive jurisdiction to the High Commission Court, as an ecclesiastical tribunal, in cases of blasphemy, apostacy from Christianity, heresy, and schism; for as much as the deciding of matters so many and of so great importance, are not within the conusance of the common law.* Caudrey's case, 5 Coke's Rep. ix. a.—As this case was in the 33d year of Elizabeth, I apprehend the authorities cited by Mr. Holt, Cro. Jac. 421. and 2 Roll. ab. 78. pl. 2. are, to say the least, dubious law: Cro. Jac. 421. Atwood's case is directly against him.

On carefully perusing in Hale's Hist. placit. Cor. ch. xxx. on heresy and apostacy, and the punishment thereof; I find, first, that by the common law of England, heresy was an offence exclusively cognizable by the ecclesiastical tribunals, either of a provincial council or the diocesan, (bishop of the diocese,) who, upon conviction, might deliver over the offender to the secular power. Vol. 1. p. 398 and 404. In conformity whereto, the statute 2 H. 4. enacted that full credence should be given to their decision hereon, p. 399.

I find, secondly, that when a person was convicted of heresy, not at common law, but under any of the statutes on this subject, which enacted a punishment *touching the life* of the offender; the judges on that ground, took cognizance *of the statute;* and on the habeas corpus assumed the right of determining, whether the heresy specifically set out in the return to their writ, was really heresy or not, as was done in Keyser's case, and Warner's case, reported Co. P. C. ch. 5. p. 42.

I find, thirdly, that in Sir M. Hale's book in the chapter above cited, there is not a sentence to show that heresy and apostacy is cognizable by the courts of common law, by indictment or information, or in any other way than by ecclesiastical authorities; save upon the return to a habeas corpus. What was then called heresy, would now be blasphemy. Offences against God, not capital at common law, are the subject of Book 1. ch. 5. of Hawkins's pleas of the crown. He enumerates them as consisting of blasphemies against God; such as denying his being or Providence, profane scoffing at the holy scripture, religious imposture, seditious words against the established religion, —which are indictable as tending to a breach of the peace! This, I presume, is one of the fictions of law, which deals wonderfully in Prosopopoeia. The authorities cited by Hawkins, are Cro. Jac. 421. directly against him. 1 Vent. 293; 3 Keb. 607; Str. 416. 788; Poph. 208; 1 Sid. 168. All comparatively recent authorities, and of little account in modern times; all of them setting aside the ancient common law; none of them relied on by Hale, and all of them founded on the absurd fiction of "tending to a breach of the peace!" If this be not legal fraud, founded on legal fiction, that is, on legal falsehood, there is no meaning in language. It appears manifestly from Hale, that the statute of 1 Eliz. under which the High Commission Court for the trial of ecclesiastical offences was appointed, did not alter the common law, but only instituted a court with defined powers to enforce it: at every stage of our investigations into a legal subject, we encounter these fictions of law; a system of mendacity that equally shocks common sense and common honesty.

Previous to Caudrey's case, however, and as a specimen of the mode of proceeding, and spirit of the times, I shall present the reader with some cases in the appendix, popish and protestant, to illustrate the odium theologicum, confined to no religion, time, or country. Luckily, increased knowledge has given a force to public opinion in Great Britain, that bids fair to preserve that country from similar disgrace in future. But the spirit of the age, in France, Spain, Austria, and Italy, that is, in the major part of Europe, is not a whit better than it was four centuries ago in England: and while I am writing, I wait constantly for the re-establishment of the jesuits and the inquisition, or some similar tribunal in France and Spain.

By 1 El. ch. 1. § 14. contemptuous words against the Lord's Supper shall be punished with fine and imprisonment.

By 1 El. ch. 2. if any minister shall speak in derogation of the common prayer book, he shall be imprisoned *a year*, for the first offence; and *for life*, for the second. And any other person, who shall speak any thing in derogation of said book, shall forfeit 100 marks for the *first* offence; 400 marks for the *second;* and for the *third,* he shall forfeit all his goods and chattels, and be imprisoned for life.

By 13 El. ch. 12. a person ecclesiastical, who shall advisedly affirm any doctrine contrary to the articles established at the convocation of 1562, is made liable to deprivation, if he persist in his error.

By 3 James 1. ch. 21. it is made indictable to use the name of the holy trinity, profanely or jestingly.

By 1 Wm. 3. ch. 18. § 11. denying the doctrine of the trinity, occasions a forfeiture of all benefit of the toleration act, and is made punishable as a misdemeanor.

By 9 and 10 Wm. 3. ch. 32. if any person educated in, or having made profession of the Christian religion, shall by writing, printing, preaching, or advisedly speaking, deny the Christian religion to be true; or the holy scriptures to be of divine authority, shall on the *first* offence, be rendered incapable to hold any office or place of trust: and for the *second,* be rendered incapable of bringing any action, being guardian, executor, legatee, or purchaser of lands, and shall suffer three years imprisonment without bail; unless within four months after the first conviction, he shall publicly renounce his error in open court, when he shall be discharged, for that once, from all disabilities.

This statute has been decided, says Mr. Holt, not to have taken away the common law punishment for the said offence. 2 Str. 834; Bernard K. B. 162; Rex v. Williams, 1797; R. v. Eaton, 1812; but I doubt this position, for it is not a common law offence. How soon after Caudrey's case, the courts of common law seized hold of jurisdiction in cases of blasphemy, I cannot distinctly trace. The first instance of a prosecution for words reflecting on religion, occurred in the 15 James 1. (Starkie on libel, 488; Cro. Jac. 421.) Atwood was convicted on an indictment for saying, "the religion now professed was a new religion within fifty years. *Preaching is but prat-*

ing; and hearing of service more edifying than two hours preaching." It was assigned for error, that this was an offence not inquirable on indictment before justices of the peace, but only before the high commissioners: and it was referred to Attorney-General Yelverton to consider thereof; and he certified, it was not inquirable before them, and of that opinion was the whole court. So that Holt's reference to this case, in his law of libel, seems not to support his position, but to oppose it.

In the King v. Taylor, Vent. 293; 3 Keb. 607. defendant was convicted on an information, for saying that "Jesus Christ was a bastard and a whore-master; "religion was a cheat; and that he neither feared God, "the devil, nor man." This person does not appear to have been in his right mind; and he should have been sent to the lunatic hospital. On this occasion, Hale, Ch. Baron, observed, that such kind of wicked and blasphemous words, were not only an offence against God and religion, but a crime against the laws, state, and government, and therefore punishable in this court, (K. B.) That to say religion is a cheat, is to dissolve all those obligations whereby civil societies are preserved; that Christianity is part and parcel of the laws of England; and therefore, to speak against religion, is to speak in subversion of law. "This is one of the hundred legal fictions "so convenient for displacing common sense, and con-"verting real falsehood into legal truth."

This appears to be the first case in which blasphemy was ruled to be cognizable in the courts of common law; and in which Christianity was determined to be parcel of the laws of England. Both of them very important innovations, and resting entirely on bench-enacted law; on Judge Hale's law. I have no respect for Sir Matthew Hale; he was a weak and bigoted man, deeply dyed with the legal servility of the times. I have before me an account published in 1682, of the trial, condemnation, and execution of *Rose Cullender* and *Amy Duny* for witchcraft, at Bury, St. Edmonds, 10th March, 1664, before Sir Matthew Hale. More satisfactory evidence of the bigoted stupidity of this judge, (after the experiment decisive of their innocence, made before himself, in open court, by Lord Cornwallis, Sir Edmond Baron, and Mr. Sergeant Keeling,) need not be produced. This gifted oracle of the bench, asserted Christianity to be part and parcel of the common law, either through gross and culpable negligence, not consulting; or through gross and culpable ignorance, misunderstanding and mistranslating a passage in the Year Book, 34 Hen. 6. fol. 38 and 40. Anno 1458, case of quare impedit, Humphrey Bohun v. the Bishop of Lincoln and others. This matter is set in its true light by Mr. Jefferson, in the letter that I have given in the appendix. Since this decision of Hale, several prosecutions have been set on foot, attended with convictions for libels on the holy scriptures and the Christian religion, which the reader may find enumerated in Starkie, chap. 31. and in the New-York edition of Holt on Libel, 77 to 81.

Since that time, and within these three or four years, the cases of Hone of Carlisle, Mrs. Carlisle, his sister Jane Carlisle, John Clarke, and others, for libels termed blasphemous, have produced an effect in England, so directly opposite to what was intended by, and expected from these prosecutions; such a spirit of hostility toward this mode of suppressing discussion; such an increase of new publications of this description; and such an increased demand for, and sale of, the publications, for which the venders have been prosecuted; that government have found it prudent to put a stop to these proceedings, and have formally remitted the fine of £1500, which had been imposed by the courts on Carlisle. These *prosecutions* have been generally considered, throughout England, as *persecutions;* and the probability is, that no jury impartially selected, could now be found to bring in a verdict of guilty on any indictment for what is called blasphemy. Folly and vulgarity are not calculated to do harm, if treated with contempt.

The spirit of investigation in England, has pervaded all ranks of the people. The populace of that country are beyond doubt, at this moment, the most reading people in Europe. The supply and sale of books there, is extensive beyond any thing that has hitherto been known in the world: and book societies, and societies for communicating mechanical knowledge, and scientific information, have been extended to almost every village in the kingdom. A body of clergy whose conduct and character are open to so many grave objections of a description but too well calculated to make the people *feel;* and a system of doctrine constituting the established religion of the country—embodying so many gross absurdities—so many positions of dubious evidence, strongly attacked, and weakly defended —so well calculated to furnish matter for dispute, and so ill calculated to promote simple, intelligible, useful morality,—form a collection of circumstances, that have undermined the root of the established religion, and the hierarchy of that country : and whenever the period of reform comes, as come it must, the whole system will, in all probability, be overturned ; and something plainer, cheaper, and more useful, like that of the United States, be substituted in its stead. It is in vain to expect that repeated admonition will ever induce the clergy of that country to commence a reform themselves. Each says, "it will last "my time, and I have but a life-estate in the system :" no consent can be obtained from them, to change the grossest errors. The bishops, soon after the close of the American war, refused their concurrence to the striking the Athanasian creed out of our book of common prayer. We have done it *here*, but the rule *there*, is,

> Touch not a cobweb in St. Paul's,
> Lest you should shake the dome!

The ground taken by the liberal party, at present, in England, (where a petition signed by two thousand members of the church establishment, has been presented within this year or two, to parliament, against prosecutions for what are called libels on religion,) is as follows:

1. Although Christianity be true, yet there are many circumstances of reasonable doubt attending its evidences, both external and internal: doubts which weigh upon the minds of some conscientious men; and which cannot be cleared away, unless the whole subject be left open to unrestrained discussion, which is the only known method of discovering and establishing truth.

2. The largest class of Christians, are the Roman Catholic. It is a known tenet of that church, that the evidences of Christianity are defective; both internal, and historical or external, unless the traditions of the church be called in aid. The protestants deny this; and assert, not without good reason, that if Christianity be not susceptible of full and reasonable proof without recurring to any such tradition, it rests upon a very unstable foundation.

3. That all the arguments hitherto adduced by the defenders of Christianity, are weakened in their efficacy and rendered suspicious, inasmuch as they have been brought forward by men hired and paid for defending it, at all events; and who, not contented with a *press* always open to them, and enormous salaries paid for their services, think it necessary forcibly to suppress the arguments of their antagonists, by calling in the aid of the civil power; by shutting against them the press; by prohibiting all means of public communication; and by *severely* punishing all doubt and denial, instead of employing reason and argument for the purpose of convincing.

4. That if a clergy maintained in Great Britain alone, during so many centuries, at the expense of at least eight millions of pounds sterling a year, with all the advantages of the very best education the country can supply, with all the countenance that the government can afford them; and all the respect that the people pay them; with the aid of bible societies, missionary societies, tract societies;—

with the concurrence too of the whole body of dissenting clergy of all descriptions, are unable to support their own tenets, and to withstand the torrent of infidelity; there must be something wrong in the cause, or something wrong in the management of it; and either the *one* should be *renounced*, or the *other altered*.

5. That a system at once so expensive and inefficient, calls aloud for reformation; and that it is high time to leave Christianity to stand or fall; to be adopted or rejected, on the strength of its own proper evidences.

In this I most cordially agree; being fully persuaded that the great number of persons who doubt of the truth of Christianity, and of persons who disbelieve it, have been thrown into this situation, owing to the unfair and persecuting manner of managing the controversy, on the part of the clergy; which furnishes prima facie evidence against the truth of the doctrines advanced. Why are these gentlemen so much afraid of trusting Christianity to its own unaided strength?

If two boys go out to fight, and one calls in the aid of a stronger boy to get the better of his antagonist, is it not clear, that he feels sure of being defeated without this assistance? So, if the priesthood fight the battle with their antagonists, by the aid of the civil power,—not confining it to the fair production of fact and argument, to be opposed to fact and argument,—but by fire and sword; by the prison and the pillory; by forfeiture, fine, confiscation, and every diabolical device of punishment, whether in a greater or a less degree,—it amounts to proof that the arguments of the unbelievers are deemed too strong for the hired advocates who oppose them, to refute; and they must call in a more able ally. This conclusion is unavoidable; and it has unfortunately been too strongly felt. It has given rise to by far the greater portion of infidelity which now exists in Europe, and which I am well persuaded, would not have existed without it to the same extent.

6. The persons who have written in favor of Christianity and its tenets, live by it: they live honored and protected as well as paid, by the government of the country, whose religion they control; and by the people, whom they instruct. The honors, the emoluments, the reputation they enjoy, are benefits of the very highest and most valuable kind that this world can offer. They have therefore a bias, a prejudice in favor of their own doctrines, that will produce a defence of them to the utmost verge of fair argument, and sometimes beyond it.

On the other hand, who are the persons who have opposed Christianity? Men who risk their reputation, their comfort, their consideration in society, their persons, their properties, the well-being of themselves, the prospects of their families, in opposition to all the power, all the wealth, all the rank and consideration prevalent in the community. And for what? Can any other reasonable motive be assigned, except that they feel desirous at all hazards, and without the possibility of recompense, to speak what appears to them the truth, on the most important of all human investigations? I grant they may be mistaken; but are these men, thus actuated and thus acting, fit objects for punishment, because they are honest, bold, disinterested, and independent? One man cheerfully goes to prison for his opinions; another receives a thousand pounds a year for teaching the opposite opinions. Which of the two would be deemed the better evidence in a court of justice?

I grant that two or three instances, (not more,) of vulgar and offensive language, proceeding from uneducated men of vulgar habits, and from the dregs of society, have been punished without commiseration: so much the worse: these cases that excite no pity, are chosen to cover and defend the practice of punishing in all cases. Moreover, it would be well for those who complain of gross and violent language, not to tempt the production of very high authority for the grossness complained of. (Vid.

Mat. ch. 23.) To show the bitter spirit with which these prosecutions were carried on, I copy the following account of one of them from the Annual Register, for the year 1820, part 1. p. 83. Surry Assizes: The King v. Philip Francis, for selling a seditious and blasphemous libel concerning the proceedings that took place in Manchester on 16th August, 1819, contained in No. 3 of Carlisle's Republican. Five counsel for the prosecution.

This is one of the great class of cases of which a great many were tried at the Middlesex sittings after last term, against different news venders. The learned King's Sergeant, Onslow, stated the case with his usual ability. It appeared that the defendant, an infirm elderly man, combines with the business of a shoemaker, at No. 13 Bermondsey-street, that of a dealer in political and other pamphlets. The libellous pamphlet in question, was published 10th September last, and sold to George Oddy, who deposed to the fact. The defendant addressed the jury to the following effect: "I am a poor ailing man; and if I "have been guilty of a crime in selling this pamphlet, I "do declare most solemnly that I did not sell it with any "wicked intention. I looked to the profits of the sale as "means of enabling me to get a living, which I found a "difficult thing to do, owing to the badness of the times, "and my own infirm state of health. As soon as I knew "that the number of the Republican in question gave "offence, I desisted from selling any more. I beg you "will not consider me as the author of the work: it is "impossible for me to read all the works I sell. Gentle-"men, I am anxious to make you believe I had no badness "of intention when I sold the pamphlet; and far was I "from thinking the sale of it would expose me to the dis-"pleasure of the Attorney-General. The moment I "understood I was acting improperly, I desisted; and I "certainly did not sell the book with any malicious or "wicked intention. If you believe this, you will acquit "me. If I have broken the law, it was without knowing

" it, because I was not aware of the tendency of the pub-
" lication, and had no design to violate the law." Called no witnesses.

" The Chief Baron charged the jury, that the defend-
" ant's intention was distinctly proved by the libel itself.
" His lordship as well as the jury, acted under the solemn
" sanction of an oath; and laying his hand on his heart,
" his lordship said, 'upon my oath, I never saw a more
" 'atrocious libel than this.' "

" The jury immediately found the defendant guilty, but
" recommended him to mercy, on account of his poverty
" and his ignorance of the nature of the libel."

" The Chief Baron: Gentlemen, are you aware how
" prejudicial such a recommendation may be? If such a
" publication as this finds its way, it will be productive
" of the most mischievous consequences. Recollect your-
" selves before you give such a recommendation. I shall
" certainly carry it into effect, as far as I can; but pray
" recollect before you give it. The jury turned round
" again in the box; and after about five minutes further
" consideration, the foreman, Benjamin Bernard, Esquire,
" said, (as we understood) My Lord, the jury are not in-
" clined to alter their opinion. The Chief Baron, *with*
" *some warmth:* then you will send all these publications
" to the most ignorant classes of society. The jury was
" composed of half special and half talesmen: the latter
" half probably under no bias, not having been selected in
" the usual way of management on these occasions."

John Caherac was then put to the bar for having sold No. 2 of the Republican, relating to the same proceedings at Manchester. His defence was, that he was a general bookseller, selling books of all kinds, both for and against government. That he had never read the pamphlet in question; but now knowing its contents, he was hostile to the doctrines contained in it. That the author being known, he the author, and not a mere seller of the pamphlet, should have been resorted to. That this was the case with Mr. Hobhouse and Sir Francis Burdett, who were the authors of alleged libels. In the one case, Mr. Stockdale, the bookseller, was discharged by the House of Commons, the author being known: and in the other case, Mr. Brooks, who had sent the libellous letter of Sir Francis Burdett, was a witness for the prosecution. The resort, therefore, should have been to the author; and not to a mere seller, who could not be presumed to know the contents of every book he sold, as was the case here. Verdict, guilty. A special jury, no doubt; selected in the usual way. This usual way of England is, to my certain knowledge, well understood in Pennsylvania, and probably in the other states.

7. It is said, and whoever will read Jeremy Bentham's discourse "Swear not at all," will think it very plausibly, perhaps, very truly said, that the supposed utility of the Christian religion, as furnishing a sanction for oaths, has been greatly overrated. The opinion begins to prevail, that all oaths of every description, in or out of courts of justice, are morally and religiously indefensible. A summary of Mr. Bentham's arguments may be seen in the 9th number of the Westminster Review. Oaths tend to detract from the immorality of simple and wilful falsehood, by making perjury alone in its legal acceptation, an object of punishment. Who in our country, refuses in a court of justice to credit a Quaker's simple affirmation? Why not punish mendacity in judicial testimony, as you now do perjury? Do so, and you will bring all kind of lying into discredit: at present, you indirectly encourage it.

8. It is asked, also,—granting the truth and necessity of the Christian religion,—where is the necessity or the propriety of employing a hired and paid ministry to teach it? Christ and his apostles preached and taught without money and without price. Freely you have received, says our Saviour, freely give. Are not the Quakers as regular attendants on public worship as any class of society whatever? Yet, no member of their society is hired and paid

for the purpose. Those who think themselves qualified and called on to deal out religious instruction, do so. They do it, to satisfy the feeling of duty. Who can value an interested, a hired, a bought, a paid religion? A religion of which the professor makes a trade and a calling; to get money by it, as he would in a lawyer's office, or at a merchant's desk? That part of the church system which requires a clergyman, who is about to enter upon a bishoprick or a living of great value, to declare solemnly, that he is moved by the Holy Ghost to accept it, has had, as it ought to have, a dreadful effect on the clerical character in England.

9. It is said, that if the simple, unmixed question were before the public, whether the Christian religion were true or false? there would be but an insignificant minority to reject it; when we consider its great and manifest superiority to every other known form of religion—the superior evidence, intrinsic and extrinsic, that accompanies it—the beautiful and simple morality inculcated in the scriptures—the manifest reformation it produced by driving before it the gross errors and practices of paganism. Few people would be backward to acknowledge this, if Christianity were confined to the plain and intelligible doctrines of our Lord himself as delivered in the four Evangelists. These are few in number, easy to be comprehended; and their practical utility is apparent upon the face of them. To the Christianity of Jesus Christ, its founder, few people would be tempted to object. What better religion can any man offer as a substitute? What better morality can a deist discover than the morality taught by Jesus Christ? What would be gained by a change? These are proper questions.

But what is Christianity? It is no longer the plain and simple system delivered by our Saviour, equally difficult to be misunderstood or disputed; but it is mixed up and involved with doctrines and fancies innumerable, unintelligible, disputable; affirmed and denied with an ignorance and virulence, as opposite to the Christianity of Jesus Christ, as light is to darkness. I omit the early dissentions of the three first centuries, the Ebionites, Marcionites, Corinthians, Manichæans, Gnostics, Donatists, Novatians, Trinitarians, Sabellians, Arians, Patripassians, Alogists, Monothelites, &c. &c. &c. What is modern Christianity? Is it Catholic or Protestant? Calvinist or Arminian? Trinitarian, Sabellian, Arian, High Arian, Low Arian, Sublapsarian, Supralapsarian, Antinomian, Universalist, Unitarian, Sandemanian, Swedenborgian, Hopkinsian, &c. &c. &c.? for all these variant sects differ from each other in some mystical tenet that they deem essential to their own ideas of Christianity. I should be glad to have known Sir Matthew Hale's precise notions of Christianity; or the learned opinions, on this subject, of Judge Kent, when it was decided in the People v. Ruggles, August, 1811, that Christianity, (the Christianity by law established in England,) was part and parcel of the law of New-York state. It is not the only instance in which we may discover that lawyers of high reputation are sometimes apt to talk without book. They are usually, indeed, content (as they may well be) with the mysteries of their own profession. Sir Matthew Hale might in reply have presented the book of common prayer: Would the New-York judges have offered the thirty-nine articles of the Episcopal church, or the Westminster confession of faith? Two documents very orthodox, no doubt, but which I have heard learned men contend, include tenets equally subversive of true religion, of common sense, of sound morality, and of social order. Of this I pretend not to judge without more attention than I am inclined to pay to an investigation so pregnant with dispute. I notice it among the other differences of theological opinion; but being satisfied myself to adhere to the few plain, useful, and undisputed doctrines which Christ himself has thought fit to deliver; I have no faith in, I ascribe no authority to, any additions, emendations, illustrations, or comments, that any other person may have thought fit to make. Of what constitutes Christianity, the sayings and precepts of Christ himself, are undoubtedly the best evidence; and in my opinion, a Christian need not look further. But on this subject, not many will think with me. Be it so. I have a right to think for myself. The Christianity, therefore, taught during 1500 years, has been confused and mixed up with human opinions: it has been changed and altered, and modified, enlarged, garbled, transformed, adulterated by human doctrines and human devices, till, at length, no one can tell what Christianity is. The bible is of no use; for each of the contending sects equally appeal to the bible. Every one defines Christianity his own way; and every one a different way: and men have been employed in murdering and tormenting each other for these fifteen hundred years, for the emolument and aggrandizement of the various orders of the Christian priesthood. Is it any wonder, under these circumstances, that infidelity should prevail? That a man who has no leisure or inclination for abstruse inquiries into a quarrelsome theology, and looking only at the surface of the question, should exclaim—"Gentlemen, "when you have settled among yourselves what you "mean by the Christian religion, I will examine as fairly "as I can, the reasons offered to me for believing it."

The man who waits till this point be amicably settled by the contending sects, must wait ad græcas calendas.

10. The enormous emoluments and the unnecessary honors conferred on the members of the hierarchy in that country, have had a baneful effect on the general reception of the state religion. The question comes before the people with the hated associations of tithes, ecclesiastical courts, birth-fees, churchings, confirmations, marriage-fees, Easter offerings, and the tribe of vexatious ecclesiastical taxes, for which no intelligible consideration is given in return. It comes associated with the notions of a body of men always voting with the court, and in hostility to

the popular voice—with palaces, revenues, dignities, and sinecures—with feasting, fox-hunting, convivial pleasures —with clerical justices of the peace, protectors of the game, and oppressors of the poor. I do not vouch for the justice or correctness of these prejudices and accusations. I know not but from publications and debates of respectable character, what degree of credit to give to them. My argument carries me no farther than to state the circumstances at present associated in that country with the national religion in the public mind. I am persuaded, after due consideration, that the services of the ecclesiastical order in Great Britain, of all kinds, are compensated, at an annual expense, of not less than forty millions of dollars of our money. Under this view of the case, it is manifest that the question of Christianity has not had fair play. People become prejudiced against it, as if religion were exclusively chargeable with all the burdens which its professors impose upon the people, under that sacred sanction. They argue against the use of Christianity, from this manifest and gross abuse of it. In this country, we are, at present, better off. Our clergy are liberally paid by the grateful contributions of their hearers; and for services rendered, satisfactory to those who pay for them. Nor are our clergy, of any description, liable to the objections made against too many of the same order in the old country. Cheerfulness, tempered with gravity, is expected every where among us; and it is seldom we find our clergy of any denomination, reproachable for neglect of moral conduct. Bigotry and intolerance are, by no means, uncommon: but they prevail most, in proportion as the clergy are ignorant, and mix little in general society. Among the presbyterians, it is said, there are many who steadily and perseveringly look to the restoration of tithes, and the establishment of a system to remunerate the clerical order, independent of the voluntary contributions of their hearers. If the people are true to themselves, and to the interests of religion, as well as to their own interests, they will crush all expectation of success to this ambitious and avaricious plan. I acknowledge myself among those who believe that Christianity will flourish most when it is not made a lucrative profession, or paid for at all. But the people have a right to do as they will with that which is their own: and if they think it becomes them to maintain a class of advocates, hired and paid for their services, I see no right that any man has to object, while he is permitted to act as he sees fit. So far as I know from past experience, or can discover from the English publications, our system works far better than theirs: and religion flourishes in proportion as it is left to take care of itself.

I have for many years been observant of the state of public opinion in Great Britain, on the subject of religion as connected with the government and the law. The well informed people of that country revolt at this connexion: they see it forcibly and cruelly maintained, not for the support of religion itself, or the promotion of the public good, but for the maintenance of a wealthy, proud, and idle class of public servants, who might be rendered more useful, (if useful they can be rendered,) at a tithe of the expense. They see that the holy alliance between church and state, is an alliance to keep the people in subjection; and to punish all attempts to expose the frauds and errors, the encroachments and the peculations of the contracting parties. It is seen that there are no other means of enlightening the public, but those furnished by open, unrestrained discussion; and that government and the priesthood well knowing this, have so modelled the doctrine of libel as to suppress inquiry, and keep the public in the dark. In this unfair attempt, they have been but too well seconded by the judicial bench of the country, who adopt as an indispensable part of their costume, the fashionable garb of loyalty and orthodoxy, essential to the court dress of the day.

The Christian religion, as taught by Jesus Christ, may

be productive of great benefit to society; it tends to render men, in all respects, more forbearing with each other; it inculcates kind feelings; it is opposed to every thing like selfishness, anger, and revenge; it adds, by means of the doctrine of a future state, an important sanction to morality: the duties it inculcates are eminently useful, simple, and intelligible. A Christian, in all respects, such as Christ has taught us to be, must be, in all respects, a better man for being so. It fulfils the great use of religion in this respect; for if a man be not made better in his dispositions, and better in his conduct, by means of the religion he professes, it is not worth professing. A religion that has no manifest effect on the *morals* of its professors, is useless to society. Any religious controversy that has no bearing on morality, is at least useless, if not a nuisance in society. Let its mutual opponents discuss it, if they please; but society is not interested in the question, excepting that the dispositions of the combatants are too often the worse for the discussion. Irritated and angry passions are brought into play, in proportion as the question is worthless. But how many good, and kind, and honest men, never think of religion at all? men who have no time to dedicate to it, who know little and care little about it, except that for form's sake, they quit their weekly labors to rest on a Sunday, whether at church with their families, or in some excursion of pleasurable relaxation? How many, (nine hundred and ninety-nine out of every thousand,) who never took the pains to investigate whether the religion they profess be true or false? who have not the leisure or the means of doing so; who are content to assume, during life, without further inquiry, the religious denomination of their parents; and who go on living honestly, wisely, and respectably, because the laws compel them to do so; because society respects and honors those who do so; because they gain, by doing so, the love and esteem of their friends and neighbors; because they find it their own interest to do so; and by habit they feel the inclination to do so. Here are good dispositions and good conduct generated and confirmed in men who think little or nothing about religion; who have no other faith but the fides carbonaria; whose profession is mere matter of accident; and who, by way of decency, comply with the usual forms. Real belief, or disbelief, therefore, is not essential to good conduct. Men may be very honest, kind, and upright, without it; though they might possibly be more so with it. This being the actual situation of society, why should we punish a man who is somewhat more inquisitive than his neighbors, because he finds reason to doubt about the theoretical question of the grounds and reasons of the Christian religion, and publishes his doubts that they may be discussed and confuted? Surely he is not worse for being seriously interested in the question, than those who never think about it at all! For mercy's sake, if he be foolish, do not add to his misfortune by punishment. Convince him (if you think it worth while) that he is in error; but convince him by argument, not by fine and imprisonment. They may produce an effect on his purse, his person, and his outward profession, but his thoughts remain as free within the prison as without. What do you gain by converting an honest unbeliever into a hypocrite? If his conduct be good, what better effect can the best religion produce? If it be bad, punish his conduct, not his opinions: you may govern the one; you cannot control the other. I assent, therefore, to what I decidedly consider as the prevailing opinion in Great Britain at the present day, except among the clergy and those connected with them: Let religion take care of itself. Infidelity will be perfectly harmless, if you do not give it the prodigious advantage which arises from the cry of persecution. Leave it to be discussed by those who feel interested in such discussions; and by and by we shall hear of infidelity no more. But if you leave a pen in the hands of one party and put a sword into the hands of the other, you may enable them to draw blood, but not to elicit truth.

I shall now briefly state what the law in this country, on the subject of religion, is. An act was passed in Pennsylvania in 1700, in Massachusetts in 1782, in New-Jersey in 1796, against speaking or writing contumeliously of the Christian religion or of the Holy Scriptures: and in the case of the People against Ruggles, 8 Johnson's Reports, 290. August, 1811, it was decided, that as the common law of England, as it prevailed in 1775, had been adopted in New-York state; as the Christian religion was part and parcel of the common law, any ridicule of Christ or of the Holy Scriptures, was an offence against the common law. Now what I object to, in this decision, is, 1st. that it is illegal: 2dly. that it is vague and vexatious.

1st. It is illegal. Mr. Jefferson's letter, which I give in the appendix, shows with what utter ignorance and negligence, the herd of judges, hypocritical and time serving, follow Sir Matthew Hale, whose authority is a mistake in translating the Norman French of the Year Book, and Prisot's opinion there reported. *There is no legal authority for Sir M. Hale's dictum.*

2dly. If the ridiculing or defaming of Christianity be blasphemy, and indictable, the public ought to be informed what is meant by Christianity, so that the offence may be avoided. Nine tenths and more of the population of New-York state, are Episcopalians or Presbyterians. Ask a person, communicant with either of these denominations, is Unitarianism Christianity? He will answer—no. Is this the state in which so important a part of the criminal law ought to be left? What is it these men mean when they talk of Christianity?

3dly. Suppose a Jew or a Mahomedan, writing in defence of his own tenets in this country, were to cast ridicule upon any part of the Scriptures, with half the freedom that we abuse Jews and Mahomedans; in England, I allow, the law, as the judges have declared it, not in conformity to, but in defiance of, early decisions, would condemn him. Would he be liable to condemnation in this country, whose constitution, as Mr. John Adams wrote to the Dey of Algiers, "is, in no sense, founded on the Christian religion?" Would this be, in the language of Mr. Jefferson, equal and exact justice to all men?

4thly. Christianity, they say, is part of the common law. When does the common law commence? Caudrey's case determines in *express words*, that blasphemy, heresy, and schism, are not cognizable at common law. This was in 33 El. Atwood's case in James 1st. settles the same question in the same way. Had Sir Matthew Hale the power of making, of enacting common law, of declaring that a case should be thenceforward part of the common law, which had never been part of it before? and that too, upon an authority which turns out to be no authority at all, except as flagrant proof of his negligence or ignorance? But the year 1700, the year 1782, the year 1796, and even the year 1811, is not the year 1830. The views of the thinking part of mankind have wonderfully changed on this and many other important subjects, within these dozen years. A bench of judges habituated to follow their leaders, may drive on, in the beaten path; but I shall be greatly mistaken if the public go with them. The angry and revengeful argument of force is fast going out of fashion; and if Christianity is to be supported, its advocates must relinquish these harsh means. If it be compelled to lean on any other prop but its own evidence, and its manifest utility, it will trust to a broken reed.

I have not pushed the argument, what is Christianity? Because I wish to abstain from all theological controversy: but it is an argument pregnant with fearful consequences, in the present vague and disgraceful state of the law on the subject: and questions might arise, and facts and arguments might be pressed on an indictment for an offence against religion, which would require more boldness and more research to determine, than judges or lawyers can bestow, who have little time to dedicate to studies so remote from tneir own.

Mr. S. Emlyn in his learned preface to the second edition of the State Trials, 1730, p. ix. makes the following important observations, to which I entirely assent. "Here "it may not be amiss to take notice of one thing relating "to the form of our indictments. It is very common to "insert words that are never meant to be proved: for "instance, the words vi et armis, (by force and arms,) in "indictments for writing and publishing libels; and in "many other cases where there is no pretence or color of "truth in them; E. G. Juratores, presentant quod I. S. "vi et armis, falsó et malitiosé scripsit quendam libellum: "which not only is an absurdity in the nature of the thing, "but tends to insnare the consciences of jurymen, who, in "giving a general verdict against the defendant, do not "always consider whether that part of the indictment be "proved. When a juryman gives a verdict against a defendant, he does in effect, declare upon oath, that he believes the entire charge as laid in the indictment to be "true: how then can he find a man guilty, generally, "when there is a part of the charge which he either believes to be false, or has no reason to believe it to be "true? It is said that these are words of course: if they "be, they still have a natural and proper meaning; else "why are they inserted? And if they are not true, I do "not see how any one can upon oath, honestly declare "they are; unless it can be thought an excuse for giving "a *rash*, not to say a *prompt* verdict,—that it is a thing "of course. These words "of course" are generally the "most material words in an indictment. *Proditoriè* is a "word of course in an indictment for treason: *burglariter* "in burglary; and *felonicè* in felony. But if any of these "words be omitted in their respective places, the indictment will be naught. It is greatly to be feared that jurymen do sometimes overlook the most essential words of "an indictment, under the notion of their being words of "course. Thus in the case of a blasphemous libel, it is "customary to insert the words *falsó et malitiosé*, *scrip-*

"*sit, &c.*, and indeed they are the very gist of the indict-
"ment, and absolutely necessary to constitute the offence;
"for as no words can be blasphemy (viz. a reproachful re-
"flection on God or religion,) which are true, (for truth
"can be no reflection on the God of truth,) so no opinion,
"however erroneous, can merit that denomination, unless
"uttered with a malicious design of reviling God or re-
"ligion. Yet how often have persons been found guilty
"on these indictments, without any proof of the falsehood
"of the positions, or of the malice of him who wrote them.
"Nay! sometimes there is a great deal of reason to think
"they were published from no other principle but a
"sincere love and regard for truth. These are things not
"always sufficiently attended to by juries. It often satisfies
"them, if the defendant be proved to have done the fact,
"viz. wrote the book, whether with the circumstances
"falsó et malitiosé, as charged in the indictment, be prov-
"ed or not. Yet when the defendant comes to move in
"arrest of judgment, that what he has done cannot amount
"to blasphemy, because it was not done with an evil in-
"tent; he is then told that it is found by the verdict, and
"must be taken to be true: and so indeed it must: but
"then it should be a caution to juries how they find a man
"guilty of an indictment, generally, without due proof of
"every part of it; since every thing which was proper for
"their consideration will, after verdict, be supposed to have
"been considered by them, whether in reality it was so
"or not.

"Thus, in the case of defamatory libels, or of scanda-
"lum magnatum, when the word falsó is inserted, the de-
"fendant ought not to be found guilty, if the assertion be
"true. Whether it be necessary to insert the word falsó
"is another question; though I believe it would be diffi-
"cult to maintain an indictment without it. Yet certainly,
"where an indictment charges a man with *falsely* writing
"a libel, he cannot justly be found guilty of that indict-
"ment so laid if the words be true."

Solomon Emlyn was the editor of Sir Matthew Hale's History of the Pleas of the Crown: and the preface from which I have made the preceding citation, Mr. Hargrave says, was much admired, and had received great and deserved commendation. As to the word *falsely* in an indictment for libel, Rex. v. Burk. v. 7. T. R. is against him; if indeed that case can be law, which I cannot admit. But the temper of the times is changed. The spirit of inquiry is abroad with the spear of Ithurial in her hand. Opinions that have long prevailed have been brought to the test of public discussion, and are hastening to oblivion: and those only that can stand that test, resting on *truth* as their basis, will preserve their influence over the public mind.

The many tenets, hard to be understood, of a jealous and quarrelsome theology, far different from the Christianity taught by Jesus Christ, will gradually disappear. They prevail only by sufferance among the well informed part of the community; and as education advances, they will retire like the shades of night before the rays of the rising sun. Whatever opinion be advanced, or whatever measure be proposed, in which society is interested, it must ere long be tried by the only criterion that society can acknowledge—UTILITY. Even *truth* itself is to be received with deference and respect, because experience has uniformly taught us that truth and utility are coincident. How is this to be ascertained if discussion be made a crime? The time is fast approaching when the manifold claims of the European priesthood will be subjected to this criterion. Whenever this happens, society will be apt to address them in the words of the hand writing on the wall, *mene, mene, tekel upharsin.* Ye are weighed in the balance, and are found wanting.

APPENDIX. NO. I.

HERESY AND BLASPHEMY.

By the ancient common law, heresy is said to have been punished by burning: so says Brook's Abrid. but there is no authority for this. Lord Commissioner Whitelock, in his defence of the poor madman, James Nayler, 1656, (2 St. Tr. case 53.) denies that any writ de heretico comburendo is to be found among any of the ancient manuscript registers. This writ first issued at the instance of Thomas Arundel, Archbishop of Canterbury, in 1401. Hen. 4th, in the case of William Sautree, who was in consequence burnt as a Lollard.—See the writ in Fitzh. Nat. brev. 594. and in p. 1. of the Appendix to the St. Tr. vol. 2. Harg. edit. 5 Rich. 2 ch. 5. is the first statute in relation to heresy; which empowers the sheriff and all other civil officers to apprehend heretics, in order to their being tried by the laws of holy Church.

It being inconvenient to summon a convocation upon every case, the stat. 2 H. 4. ch. 15. empowers the Diocesan to inquire and proceed; and on conviction and contumacy, to deliver the offender to the secular power, (to be burned.)

2 H. 5. ch. 7. All civil officers are required to aid the ordinary in extirpating heresy.

25 H. 8. ch. 14. requires that no one shall be subjected to this punishment, except where the writ de heretico comburendo shall first have issued.

1 and 2 Phil. and Mar. reviving 5 R. 2. St. 2 ch. 5. and 2 H. 4. ch. 15. touching the arresting of heretical preachers, and repressing of heretics, and punishment of

heresy, are repealed by 1 El. ch. 1. sect. 15. This act repealing some, and reviving other acts relating to ecclesiastical affairs, abolishes all foreign authority, spiritual and temporal; and by § 18, enables her majesty, her heirs and successors, to appoint fit persons to visit, reform, redress, order, correct, and amend all errors, heresies, schisms, abuses, offences, contempts, and enormities, which fall under the spiritual and ecclesiastical power, authority, and jurisdiction. This is the origin of the High Commission Court, afterwards appointed in 26 Eliz. Dec. 29th.

§ 36 confines heresy to what has been so declared by either of the *four* first general councils, or by any other general council, from the express and plain words of the canonical scriptures; or that may be determined hereafter to be heresy by Parliament, with the assent of the clergy in convocation. None to be convicted but on the oaths of two witnesses.

1 Eliz. ch. 2. is the act of uniformity of common prayer and church service, &c.; punishing by fine and imprisonment, any thing spoken in derogation of the common prayer; ordering attendance of all people at church on Sundays and holydays.

By 29 Ch. 2. ch. 9. 1680, the writ de heretico comburendo, and all capital punishments for ecclesiastical censures were abolished; so that heresy now only incurs the punishment of excommunication.

It may be worth while to give some instances of the kinds of heresy and blasphemy, that have been punished with death, or in some other violent and cruel manner, by the clergy, for the time being, from 1400 to the revolution of 1688.

1 St. Tr. p. 20. 1407, William Thorpe came into the town of Shrewsbury, and thorow leave granted him to preach, he did openlye say in his sermon at Synt Chaddis Chirche,

That the sacrament of the altar after consecration, was material brede (bread,)—[The prevailing popish opinion then being, that consecration totally changed the material bread that was, into the body of Christ.]

That ymages sholde in no wise be worshipped.

That men sholde not go on pilgrimages.

That priests have no title to tithes.

That it is not lawful to swear in any wise.

On being accused thereof by Thomas Arundel, Archbishop of Canterbury, he seems to have endeavored to explain away the obvious meaning of these propositions. He proposed that the clergy should be maintained by the voluntary contribution of their hearers, (p. 29.) For in reply to the question, Do you say that the priesthood have no title to tithes? He said—"Syr, if priests were "now in mesurable mesure and numbre, and lived virtu- "ously, and taught besyly (industriously) and truly the "word of God, by example of Christe and his apostles, "withouten tythes, offeryngges, and other dewties that "priests do now challenge and take, the people wolde "gyve them freely sufficient lyvelihood." To which the Archbishop said with great spirite,—Goddis (God's) curse have thou and thyne for this teaching. He was remanded to prison, where he died. Were these dreadful heresies now charged upon me, I sadly fear I should be tempted to plead guilty to all of them.

The case of Sir John Oldcastle, Lord Cobham, came on 23d Sept. 1413, 1 Hen. 5. The report of it (1 St. Tr. 41.) contains a kind of creed of the church of that day, which it may be worth while to compare, so far as it goes, with the Roman Catholic profession of the modern Irish reformers.

This is the determination of the Archbishop and clergye, on his first examination.

The faith and determination of the holy Church, touching the blessful sacrament of the aulter, is this: That after the sacramental words once spoken by a priest in his masse, the material bread, that was before bread, is turned into Christe's very body; and the material wyne, that was before wyne, is turned into Christe's very blood: and so there remayneth in the sacrament of the altar, from thensforth, no material bread, or material wyne, which were there before the words spoken.

Holy church hath determined that every Christian man lyving here bodyly uppon earth, ought to be shriven (confessed) to a priest ordeyned by the church, if he may come to him.

Christ ordeyned Sainct Peter, the apostle, to be his Vicar here on earth, whose See is the Holy Church of Rome: and he graunted that the same power which he gave to Peter, should succeed to all Peter's successors, which we now call Popes of Rome. By whose special power in churches particular, he ordained prelates, as Archbishops, Bishops, Parsons, Curates, and other degrees more, whom Christen men ought to obey, after the laws of the Church of Rome.

Holy church hath determined that it is merytorious to a Christen man to go on pilgrimage to holy places; and there especially to worship holy relyques and ymages of saintes, apostles, martyrs, confessors, and all other saintes besydes, approved of the church of Rome.

To each of which propositions, Sir John Oldcastle was asked "how fele ye this article?" He was excommunicated, and delivered over to the secular arm to be punished as an heretic convict. [In 1535, Sir Thomas Moore, then Chancellor, was convicted of high treason, for denying the king's ecclesiastical supremacy. This he had no right to complain of, having been chiefly instrumental in causing two men to be put to death for what he called heresy.]

In case of a warrant to apprehend a heretic, it must set out the heresies of which he was accused. So in the case of Bartholomew Legatt, 9 James 1st, 1611, (Appendix to the 2d vol. of St. Tr.) who was condemned and burnt as a heretic; the warrant states thirteen heretical opinions held by the said Bartholomew Legatt, viz:

1. That the Nicene and Athanasian creeds do not contain a true profession of Christian faith.

2. That Christ is not God, of God begotten, not made; but begotten and made.

3. That there are no persons in the Godhead.

4. That Christ was not God from everlasting, but only when he took flesh from the Virgin Mary.

5. That the world was not made by Christ.

6. That the apostles teach Christ to be man only.

7. That there is no generation in God; but of creatures.

8. That to say God was made man, is horrible blasphemy.

9. That Christ was not before the fulness of time, except by promise.

10. That Christ was not God otherwise than anointed God.

11. That Christ was not in the form of God, equal with God; that is, in substance of God, but in righteousness, and giving salvation.

12. That Christ by his Godhead, wrought no miracle.

13. That Christ is not to be prayed unto.

For which "most dangerous, blasphemous, damnable, "and heretical opinions," he was pronounced and condemned to be an obstinate and incorrigible heretic; and delivered over to the secular power, whence a writ de heretico comburendo issued: and he was duly burnt in West Smithfield, according to the clerical fashion of that day.

It would be very difficult to say of what possible use or detriment, the belief or disbelief of these abstruse and enigmatical propositions could be to society. I greatly object to burning a man for talking nonsense, and wasting his time unprofitably; else many well-meaning persons would run the hazard of making their exit, like Legatt, who were, in all other respects, very worthy men and good citizens. If a man may believe or disbelieve, either side of a proposition, without affecting his character as a dutiful son, a faithful husband, a careful father, a good citizen, a kind neighbor, and an honest man, why meddle with his belief or disbelief?

In 1618, John Selden, the most learned man of his day, published "a history of tithes," in which he seemed to combat the divine right of the church to them, and consequently gave great offence to the clergy, and incurred the displeasure of King James. In a short time he was cited before the High Commission Court; his book was prohibited, and he was enjoined to declare his contrition for having written it, and was forbidden, on pain of imprisonment, to reply to any person who might write against it. "Wood" says that the usage he met with, sunk so deep into his stomach, that he did never after affect the bishops and clergy, nor cordially approve their calling, though many ways were tried to gain him to the interest of the church.—Seldeniana, Pref.

The protestants complain of the intolerance, the bigotry and cruelty of the Roman Catholics! *Clodius accusat mæchos, Catalina Cethegum.* What a complete and satisfactory way of arriving at truth it is, to prohibit all discussion; and admit of no argument, but in favor of one side of the question! This is, however, the *modern*, as well as *ancient* practice of the clergy; who consider truth as their most inveterate foe: perhaps they are right.

I am afraid "the learned Selden," as he is always termed, was not so orthodox as he might have been. Speaking of the clergy, he says, "They would have us "believe them against our own reason, as the woman "would have had her husband against his own eyes. "What, (says she) would you believe your eyes before "your own sweet wife?" Seldeniana voce Clergy.

2 St. Tr. 550. Oct. 1664, 16. ch. 2d. Benjamin Keach was indicted for a libel, inasmuch as he had published in "The Child's Instructer, or new and easy Primer," to wit, the following blasphemous doctrines among others,

viz. : " Christ hath not chosen the wise and prudent men " after the flesh, nor great doctors and rabbis ; not many " mighty and noble, saith Paul, are called, but rather the " poor and despised ; even tradesmen and such like, as " was Matthew, Peter, Andrew, Paul, and others. And " Christ's true ministers have not their learning and wis- " dom from men, or universities, or human schools of " human learning. Arts and sciences are not essential to " the making of a true minister, but the gifts of God, which " cannot be bought with silver or gold : also as they have " freely received the gift, so do they freely administer. " They do not preach for hire or gain, or filthy lucre. " They are not like the false teachers who look for gain " from their quarter; who eat the fat and clothe them- " selves with the wool, and kill them that are fed : those " that put not into their (the false teachers') mouths, they " declare war against : also, they are not lords over God's " heritage; they rule them not by force and cruelty; " neither have they power to force and compel men to " believe, but are only to persuade and entreat: for this " is the way of the gospel, as Christ taught them."

This being expressly in opposition to the emoluments and power of the clergy and the pretensions of a hired and paid priesthood, it is no wonder he was convicted. He was fined £20, and stood in the pillory two hours.

Jan. 1679, 2 St. Tr. p. 992. Anderson, and six other priests were indicted under an old statute, 27 Eliz. ch. 2. § 3. ninety-three years old, for high treason ; *in remaining and abiding in the realm of England*, contrary to the statutes thereof. Convicted. Sentence, to be hanged, cut down alive, to have their privy members cut off, their bowels taken out, and burned before their faces! And yet protestants complain of popish cruelty !

Lord Commissioner Whitelock, in his speech in favor of James Nayler, mentions a case where the bishop committed a man for heresy, "for denying that tithes were due "to the parson." 2 St. Tr. 275. Proof in abundance can be produced, that the *same denial* is treated as heresy by many *presbyterian* preachers and writers of the present day.

When people grew tired of burning heretics, and the writ de heretico comburendo was no longer permitted to gratify the clerical thirst for blood, the judges took up the subject of blasphemy, which is defined to be "a malicious "reviling of God or the holy scriptures." The maxim of the ancient pagans was *injuriæ deorum diiscuriæ.* The gods will take care to punish injuries committed against themselves. But the holy zeal of the Christian church seems to think that the Deity is too negligent; that heretics and blasphemers may be carelessly overlooked in the next world; or that the punishment of eternal damnation there, will not suffice without due punishment in this world also. I would ask, is it possible for any man, who believes in the existence of a God at all, seriously and wilfully to revile or insult him? I cannot conceive it possible. A man may disbelieve, or make complaints of an overruling Providence from a consideration of the existence of so much moral evil in the world; but as to reviling or insulting the Supreme Being, wilfully and maliciously, I do not believe it ever happened with any man, however depraved. But in another point of view the offence is impossible. If any thing be blasphemy, it is blasphemy against the attributes of the Deity, to suppose that he can be affronted at any thing said by a poor, weak being, whom he has created and permits to exist. Can a worm crawling on the ground, insult the Supreme Being? I wish these persecutors would read Dr. Franklin's chapter on toleration. "Have I not borne with him for these "four-score years,—and cannot you bear with him for "one hour?" If any thing be blasphemy, it is to attribute all our own weak, wicked, and revengeful passions to the Deity, as if he were a proud, cruel, jealous, and unforgiving tyrant, as weak and as wicked as the bench of bishops or the bench of judges. If any persons ought to be punished, it is those violent zealots, who clothe Christianity in the garb of a fury, ready to cry "havoc, and let "loose the dogs of war!" Yet to these fiery Christians have legislators and lawyers lent a willing ear and willing aid: and mistakes, and mere differences of opinion, in themselves as innocent as the belief or disbelief of Abracadabra, have been converted into crimes; and punishments have been inflicted on men for being guilty of a mere dissent from popular opinion, and for assigning their reasons for this dissent. A crime so called, which could not have been committed but from honest and upright motives, by men really seeking for truth.

The real crime rests with the hired, and paid, and bigotted persecutors; not with the men whose very criminality, as charged upon them, completely negatives all selfish and interested motives, however mistaken they may be. Those are not the real friends to Christianity, who declare aloud to the world, that it cannot stand without the aid of the civil authority, and secular punishments to support it; that unless its opponents be silenced by fine and imprisonment, and all other kind of direct and indirect persecution, it must fall; for that no other reply, satisfactory to the public, can be given to the arguments by which it is assailed! What need then, if such be the case, of such prodigious numbers of clergymen of all descriptions? Idlers, who prey on the pockets of the people, and who are maintained at an expense so enormous! If two chymists or mathematicians quarrel, do they mutually apply to a magistrate to send their antagonist to jail? *A la lanterne*, cried the mob, when they had seized the Abbé Maury. *Et bien mes amis* (said he,) *en seriez vous plus eclairé.* No argument so forcible, so conclusive, has ever been brought against Christianity, as this cowardly conduct of its hired advocates; this manifest proof of conscious weakness; this dread of fair discussion; this resort to the sword of the law, in lieu of opposing fact to fact, and argument to argument, that truth may appear in all her brightness, like pure gold out of the refiner's furnace.

Within these last fifty years, human intellect has received an impulse much stronger than at any former similar period within the history of literature. Every subject has been brought before the tribunal of the public, and subjected to severe examination. Error has not been sheltered, because it is ancient error; and a more solid, bold, and manly style of thinking, on every known subject of human inquiry, has been the result. Christianity has come in for its share in the discussions of the time, and objections have been made too grave to be passed over, until the indolent security of the well fed hierarchy in England became roused. But prosecutions for blasphemy, were easier and more effectual arguments than replies from the press, in the fair but laborious method of literary discussion. During the whole reign of George the third, and under every administration but the present, indictments were brought, and convictions procured against the authors and publishers of attacks on the Christian religion, under the old decisions against blasphemy. The general pretence, wherever it could be set up, was the vulgarity and insolence of the offenders; forgetting the zealous protestants' abuse of the Jews, and their polite denunciations of the great scarlet whore, that sitteth on seven hills, playing the harlot, and making the people drunk with her abominations. They appear not to be aware, that hard and harsh language against what is deemed imposture and hypocrisy, is not only their own language, but is in fact countenanced by 23 Mathew, and 23 Acts. They forgot that it is unjust to expect the mild language of a well educated gentleman from those who have been accustomed to vulgar society; and who express what they deem honest feelings, in the terms they have unfortunately been accustomed to hear, and to use. They forgot that there is no known or precise law for indicting mere coarseness of language; especially in persons whose previous education forbids us to expect any other. Forgetting all these considerations of prudence; forgetting their own indulgence in the most violent and vulgar abuse of Jews, Papists, Infidels, and Hereticks; the Orthodox party went on, accusing and indicting, until they pitched upon a printer of no education, but of determined and persevering spirit, of the name of *Richard Carlisle.* He was indicted and convicted as the seller of Paine's Age of Reason, a book written by a reflecting, well meaning, and honest man; which ought to have been refuted instead of being prosecuted. The reply to that book by Bishop Watson, though not conclusive, did great credit to the latter, and great service to the cause he defended. The prosecutions against Paine's Age of Reason have extended the sale of it to 50,000, and done great mischief to Christianity in England, because these prosecutions put on the semblance, not of fair reply, but of persecution. In this country the exclamations against Paine, for expressing opinions which he had a right to express, (but which would have been little noticed by the public, but for the silly outcry raised against him,) have caused the circulation of many thousand copies, which would otherwise have been waste paper. The best thing the clergy can do, will be to publish Paine's Age of Reason, and Bishop Watson's excellent and temperate reply together; and then let the people judge for themselves.

Under various indictments, Carlisle was confined for six years, in Dorchester jail, and fined £1500. His shop was then conducted first, by his wife, while he was in prison: she was indicted, convicted, and imprisoned: then by his sister. The same proceedings were instituted against her; and she was also convicted. Then succeeded one of his journeymen, John Clarke, who was indicted and imprisoned in Newgate; whence he has issued another book of the same description with Paine's, consisting of letters to the commentator Dr. Adam Clarke, on the internal evidence of Christianity. To him succeeded others of Carlisle's adherents, to the number of nine.* Meanwhile the sale

* On June 7th, 1824, Old Bailey Sessions, Mr. Carlisle's journeymen, to the number of nine, were brought up to plead to indictments for selling

of these obnoxious publications continued increasing at an alarming rate; and the prosecuting party began to perceive, that they were doing more harm than good to their own cause, by these proceedings; and desisted. On the 30th June, 1825, Mr. Brougham presented the following petition to the House of Commons, on behalf of Carlisle.

Petition of RICHARD CARLISLE, a prisoner in Dorchester jail, to the Honorable the Commons of Great Britain and Ireland, in parliament assembled, showeth,

That since the year 1818, your petitioner and about twenty other persons have been prosecuted, at what is called common law, for blasphemy toward the Christian religion.

That on the 16th day of November 1819, your petitioner was sentenced by the Court of King's Bench, to three years imprisonment in Dorchester jail, and to fines of £1500, as the consequences of this prosecution.

That your petitioner has never been able to see, that he has been dealt with according to law; and is possessed of very strong arguments to show that such has not been the case: but that having been deprived of all his property, by seizures for his fines, in addition to his continued imprisonment for near six years, he has never since possessed the means to proceed for justice, by writ of error.

That there exists a statute passed in the year 1813, entitled "an act to relieve those persons who impugn the

Paine's Age of Reason, Palmer's Principles of Nature, and the Republican. Six were tried. The conduct of the court, the jury, and the advocates, on both sides, was, by no means, such as to excite respect, either for fairness or intelligence. The fall of the hierarchy in that country is certain. The proceedings against Carlisle and his followers, will assuredly hasten it. Carlisle was supported in prison by weekly contributions, all over the kingdom, of very small sums. Much of the conduct and opinions of this bold and intrepid man I cannot approve; but the vice society, and the clergy, have acted very imprudently by this virulent persecution of him, and his adherents; and have shown that although they may be very orthodox subjects, they are any thing but Christians.

"doctrine of the Holy Trinity,"* which statute plainly and expressly relieves those who impugn the Trinity, from all pains and penalties.

That the doctrine of the Trinity being the foundation of the Christian religion, as it has been previously recognised by the law of England, to impugn that doctrine is, according to your petitioner's judgment, to blaspheme the Christian religion as previously established by law; and that this statute was, as plain as words could make it, a repeal of all former power of the law to interfere with the religion of the country.

That your petitioner pleaded this law in the Court of King's Bench, as his justification; but was answered that the common law† was paramount to it.

That your petitioner cannot understand how two laws can justly exist in the same country, the one hostile to the other; or how the common law can declare that to be a crime, which the statute law has declared to be no crime: and he finds himself unwarily entrapped in an alleged law, of the existence of which he has no knowledge, under the conclusion which he thought himself entitled to make, that the latest made law repealed all prior opposition.

That it appears by reports of public proceedings, that the highest law officer in the country has alarmed a large body of the people, (who thought themselves secure in the statute law) by the assertion, that they are criminals in the eye of this alleged common law.

That the allegation, that Christianity was, or is, part or parcel of the law of the land; and that to impugn it was or is an offence at common law, was first asserted by Sir Matthew Hale, without reference to any precedent of prior authority.‡

* By act of parliament, 1713, it is declared to be blasphemous and punishable, to impugn the doctrine of the Holy Trinity.

† Caudrey's case. Co. Rep. is directly contrary to this law of the court.

‡ See on this subject, Mr. Jefferson's unanswerable review of the modern doctrine.

That but a few years before this unfair addition to the common law, Lord Chief Justice Coke, always considered as good an authority as Sir Matthew Hale, distinctly laid it down as law, in mentioning the case of Caudrey,—" So in causes ecclesiastical and spiritual, as blasphemy, apostacy from Christianity, heresies, schisms, &c., *the conusance whereof belongeth not to the common law of England;* the same are to be determined and decided by ecclesiastical judges, according to the king's ecclesiastical laws of this realm:" and he gives as a reason, " for as before it appeareth, the deciding of matters so many, and of so great importance, is not within the conusance of the common law."

That before the abolition of the Star Chamber, and the decay of the ecclesiastical courts, no cases of blasphemy towards the Christian religion were known to the common law courts.

That no statute can be found, which has conferred authority on the common law courts, to take conusance of a charge of blasphemy toward the Christian religion, as assumed by Sir Matthew Hale.*

That it therefore clearly appears, that, *that* and the subsequent conusance of such cases by the common law courts, have been an unjust usurpation of power, and an unlawful creation of law, contrary to the common and statute laws of this realm.

That later, in the middle of the 18th century, Lord Mansfield decided that the common law did not take conusance of matters of opinion: whence it appears by

* Sir Matthew Hale cannot escape the charge of gross and culpable ignorance. There is no authority for his dictum but the references in Finch, Wingate, and Brooke, to the *ancient scripture, old records* of Prisot, in Bohun v. the Bishop of Lincoln. I have carefully examined this case, and also Brooke and Wingate. Mr. Jefferson's account of the progress of this fraud on the people is correct. The modern doctrine is, throughout, mere bench-legislation, arising from manifest fraud or manifest ignorance; and in no respect founded on common, or on statute law. Let any modern judge answer, if he can, Mr. Jefferson's view of the subject.

this, and by the authority of Lord Coke, the immediate predecessor of Sir Matthew Hale, that the judges are not unanimous on this subject; and that Sir Matthew Hale evidently warped the common law to punish an individual who had not committed an infringement of that or of any other law; and that such has been the conduct of the judges in the case of your petitioner and others.

That as the Roman Catholic sect of the Christian religion was alone known to the common law,—that as no addition can have been justly made to the common law, since the reformation from that religion,—that since the existing statute laws pronounce the religion of the common law to have been and to be "idolatry and damnable,"—and since the act of 1813, which allows the doctrine of the Trinity to be impugned: (to impugn, meaning the assertion of its falsehood; to speak evil of, or to blaspheme, or to try to overthrow)—it is clear, that the existing religion of the statute law is not recognised or recognisable by the common law of the country.

That upon these grounds and arguments your petitioner feels that he has not been dealt with according to law; and that he has been grievously fined and imprisoned contrary to law: and he therefore prayeth, that your honorable house will give him relief, by the investigation of his case, or by restoring to him the property of which he hath been deprived, on pretence of seizing for his fines, to enable him to proceed by writ of error.

RICHARD CARLISLE.

Dorchester Jail, June 24th, 1825.

This petition was supported by Mr. Brougham, who presented it. None of the law officers of the crown spoke upon the subject, or attempted to controvert any of the positions stated by the petitioner. The king's warrant for remission of the fine unpaid, imposed on Richard Carlisle, is dated 12th November, 1825. The warrant for the remission of the sureties, is dated 16th November, 1825. Mr. Brougham's conduct on this occasion, was in conformity to that noble passage in his inaugural address at Glasgow, printed at the request of the principal, professors, and students of that University; and of course adopted by them. "*The great truth has finally gone* "*forth to all the ends of the earth,* THAT MAN SHALL NO "MORE RENDER AN ACCOUNT TO MAN, FOR HIS BELIEF, "OVER WHICH HE HAS HIMSELF NO CONTROL. *Hence-* "*forward nothing shall prevail upon us to praise or to* "*blame any one for that which he can no more change,* "*than he can the hue of his skin or the height of his* "*stature.*"

The following observations by Carlisle, 12 Repub. 652. are in point.

"Before an irreligious book can be proved to be ill "founded and mischievous, the religion it attacks must be "proved to be well founded and not mischievous. This "is a question of fair and free discussion, but not for per- "secution: for whatever the former decides will be suf- "ficient, without the latter, which can decide nothing.

"Again. What is the Christianity, which is part and "parcel of the law of England? The judges of the Court "of King's Bench, when pressed, said it was part of the "common law. The common law is elsewhere defined "as that, to which the memory of man runneth not to the "contrary. A line has been drawn for the common law; "that it is a principle of law which existed before Richard "the First. Now, the Christianity that existed before "that time, was the Christianity of the Roman Catholic "Church; and that Roman Catholic Christianity, the "present English church, as by law established, pro- "nounces 'idolatrous and damnable.' The legislature, or "the statute law of 1713, pronounced it blasphemous and "punishable to impugn the doctrine of the holy Trinity, "—doctrine of a Christian Deity. The legislature, or the "statute law of 1813, pronounced it lawful to impugn the "doctrine of the holy Trinity, the doctrine of a Christian "Deity. What then is the Christianity which is a part and "parcel of the law of England? What is Christianity in this "country of sects and schisms? We know what it is in "Spain, in Portugal, at Rome; but what is it in England? "since that of Rome has been declared to be idolatrous "and damnable. Hence no one can understand what is "meant by blasphemous publications, or by Christianity: "and, what no one can understand, no law can justly take "cognizance of, or support."

However mistaken Richard Carlisle may be in the opinions he publishes, he is beyond doubt an honest, undaunted, persevering defender, in theory and in practice, of the inestimable privilege of *free discussion*, to whatever question it may be applied, sacred or profane. No man opposes this right; no man questions it, but from dishonest and cowardly motives. Every man who honestly seeks for truth, allows it to his antagonist, and insists on it for himself. They oppose it, and *they only*, who stand in dread of confutation, and who fear the truths it is calculated to elicit. The disputant who objects to it, is assuredly in the wrong; and his fears betray the weakness of his cause. What are we to say to the bravery of men who are quite anxious to fight, provided their antagonists be hand-cuffed? Even where the laws prohibit this advantage to be taken, the clergy and their adherents set up the hue and cry of mad-dog against all who oppose their contradictory and unintelligible dogmas; or their schemes of ambition, avarice, and imposition. As yet the majority of every community upon earth are, comparatively, unenlightened. They follow the path of their fathers, without looking on either side; and adopt the tenets of their parson without investigation. When instigated by their clerical guides, they take accusation for proof; and difference of opinion for crime; and are too prone to join in all kinds of indirect persecution which positive law is unable to repress: and if they cannot hang, fine, or imprison, they are ready to support, by all indirect means, the rancorous outcries of the clergy, against any and every person who exposes the unwarrantable pretensions of that most dangerous body of men. We have seen, and we yet see too much of this in our own country. However, science and knowledge are increasing; and where the press is tolerably free, imposition of every kind must gradually lose ground. Education, therefore, and the diffusion of useful publications, are the slow but sure remedies for an evil which, for another half century, we must bear with patience. The general establishment of book societies and reading rooms in every village and country town, throughout the Union, would do infinite good here, as similar institutions, by voluntary subscription, have done in Great Britain. The evils I complain of, I consider as emanating from that abuse of the practice and commands of Jesus Christ,—*a hired, and paid, and salaried priesthood.*—" Freely ye have received, (said our " Saviour,) freely give." But the teachers of religion every where, but among the Quakers, embrace the profession of preachers, not moved by the Holy Ghost, not for the salvation of souls, not to propagate the gospel, but as a means of livelihood; like a lawyer, a doctor, or a schoolmaster. Their aim, therefore, is not the gospel, but the money it produces: and they strive to their utmost to verify the saying—" Godliness is great gain."

In the year 1819, Mr. William Lawrence, F. R. S. and Lecturer at the Royal College of Surgeons, published his lectures on *physiology, zoology, and the natural history of man.* Mr. Lawrence was not only a surgeon and anatomist of the highest reputation, but far better acquainted than his cotemporaries, with the works of the continental philosophers on the same subject. His lectures, therefore, comprised a body of information no where else to be found in our language, digested with great skill and care. In these lectures, (sect. iv. p. 104–115.) he expressed the opinion held by at least nine-tenths of the physiologists of Europe, as well as of our own country, that man is one uniform being, not compounded of a soul and a body, each of them capable of a separate existence, distinct from the other, and that when the body dies the soul survives; but that all the phenomena of mind or intellect, from whence we deduce the separate existence of a soul, are really bodily phenomena, dependent on the organization and properties of the nervous system excited to action. This is fairly deducible, as the opinion of Cabanis, of Blumenbach, of Rush, of Richerand, of Majendie, of Adelom; all of whose writings form the elementary collection which young physicians and physiologists study in England and in this country. I have had occasion, of course, to examine for myself, the same question. Not satisfied with a laborious investigation of this subject, physiologically and metaphysically, I went to the scriptures, not for the purpose, and hardly with the expectation, of finding it there; but as I can well aver, with all honesty, for the purpose of ascertaining what opinions on this subject were really inculcated there. I was in search of truth wherever I could find it. The result has fully satisfied me, that materialism is the doctrine of the Old Testament; that it is the doctrine of the apostles, and of the Christian fathers generally, during the four first centuries after Christ. But I put these authorities out of the question. I go to the head of the spring. I aver without the slightest doubt or hesitation, that what is now usually exclaimed against, as materialism, and considered as heresy and blasphemy, by men who are ignorant and bigoted, (because they never read their bibles with due care,) is really, plainly, and demonstrably, the doctrine held and taught by *Jesus Christ himself*, if the evangelists have given a true account of him. I want no other proof than the four evangelists supply: and I would desire the question to be confined to them, as affording the best and highest evidence of what Jesus Christ said and did: it is manifest, all other evidence is second-hand. I do not wonder at the modern clergy holding the contrary doctrine, because they received it traditionally from the

Church of Rome, to which it has been an engine of power, over weak minds most powerful, and a doctrine most lucrative. Indeed, it is to be expected that the clergy sit down to their bibles, for the most part, not to find what doctrines are really delivered there, but to find proofs of the opinions which they are hired and paid for preaching and teaching. With serious and impartial Christians, I consider myself upon perfectly safe ground. After all, the doctrine of a soul or no soul, is a matter to a Christian of practical indifference; a doctrine of mere curiosity. Let it be granted that there is a future state, which no Christian denies; and that men are to be rewarded and punished hereafter according to their conduct in this life. Is it of any practical consequence to a man who thus believes in a future state, whether the rewards and punishments shall be applied to a body raised from the dead for the purpose, (as the scriptures teach,) or to a soul which has never been raised at all, because being immortal, it has never died; and which the scriptures most assuredly do not countenance? In either case, the religious sanction for good conduct is the same: and the determination of the question is of no practical moment. It is the man that lived and died, who will be raised, punished or rewarded. How can that be raised from the dead, which being incapable of death, has never died? Good men and serious Christians have believed on the disputed point, both ways; and may do so, without impeachment of their religious character. It is of infinite importance to Christianity, a system in itself so simple, so useful, that nothing should be considered essential to it, about which there can be any reasonable doubt. The doctrines delivered by Christ himself, admit of none; they are few in number, easy to be understood, and of manifest utility to mankind. Self-conceited commentators have made of Christianity a senseless jargon, impossible to be understood; which reasonable men are compelled to reject as neither useful nor true. Christianity will have its proper effect on those only, who believe, after reasonable examination, and upon reasonable conviction.

The doctrine of a separate soul had been rejected openly by Dr. Edmund Law, Archdeacon of Carlisle and Master of Peter's College, Cambridge; father of Lord Ellenborough: and was considered by Dr. Watson, Bishop of Landaff, as a subject of reasonable doubt, in his preface to a collection of tracts compiled by him *for the use of young clergymen.* These dignitaries of the church were never called to account for this article of their creed; nor did any one venture to attack their arguments. Afterwards, Dr. Priestly, who was as fully persuaded of a future state of rewards and punishments, as he was of his existence, published a labored refutation of the doctrine of a separate soul; but he was never called to account for this opinion. It is well known that Dr. Rush of Philadelphia, held the same sentiments. Lawrence's very modest and brief view of the subject, was delivered as the result of physiological investigation, without any view to its theological bearing; and certainly not as a new opinion. These previous observations are necessary to show the indefensible character of the persecution, which this very learned and able man has undergone, and which the clergy are still pursuing with a malevolence devoid of all foresight. Thank God! their conduct bids fair to exemplify the proverb,—*Quem deus vult perdere, prius dementat.* Be it so.

On the publication of his book, Mr. Lawrence was deprived of his professorship, on the pretence that his opinions advanced in it, were in disparagement of the Christian religion. So it is that silly men, pretending to be Christians, read their bibles! or rather do never read their bibles: if they did, they would have found full support for Mr. Lawrence's opinions, in the opinions of our Saviour himself. These circumstances added to the intrinsic merit of the book, occasioned it to be much in request. In consequence of which, it was pirated by one Smith, a bookseller in the Strand, and being printed in an inferior manner, sold at a cheaper rate than the original edition. Mr. Lawrence applied to the Chancellor, Lord Eldon, for an injunction to stop the sale of the pirated edition, as being a fraud upon himself and his publisher. Smith's counsel took the objection,—that as every man asking the aid of a court in support of his rights, must exhibit an unobjectionable case on his own part, Mr. Lawrence was not entitled to relief, inasmuch as there were opinions advanced in the book in question, derogatory to our holy religion. (All the lawyers of England, who look forward to preferment, are purists, and trim their religious garments to the very straitest fashion of orthodoxy, as held by the bench.)

Lord Eldon, whose head is stuffed so full of law that no corner is left for common sense to occupy as a resting place, was delighted with this quibble. He determined that no man should be suffered to write any thing that tended in derogation of our holy religion: that the doctrine of materialism was a blasphemous doctrine: that even though he might entertain a doubt whether an opinion was excusable or not, yet he had no right to give his concurrence to the publication, while he even doubted of the propriety of so doing: that Mr. Lawrence's counsel, under these circumstances, could take nothing by the motion.

From the very first commencement of legal absurdity, dating from time whereof the memory of man runneth not to the contrary, even unto the present day, never was any opinion judicially delivered, so perfectly felo de se, of its own intention. The mischief to be remedied, was the propagation of books containing opinions hostile to our holy religion: the intention was to throw obstacles in the way of the publication and sale of such books: and the remedy was, giving license to every scoundrel in the community to disseminate the publication far and wide, ad libitum, by means of cheap editions, till the public could take off no more! The bar stood aghast at this manifest inconsistency. Smith's counsel were astounded at their own success!

But this was not the only objection to which this strange decision was liable. The Court of Chancery is a court instituted peculiarly for the suppression of fraud. In the present case, the court permits a man to be injured, who might have published an obnoxious opinion, with an honest intention, which every one allowed was Lawrence's case, in favor of another man, *who could not have acted* from any motive but a fraudulent one.

Again. The Chancellor sets himself up as witness, judge, and jury, of what is, or what is not, derogatory to religion. His business was to have recommended the Attorney-General, or the vice-society, or any other friend of orthodoxy, to prosecute the author for blasphemy. After conviction, but surely not before, he would have a legal right to say this is blasphemous, and to have enjoined both editions. But to say off-hand and without inquiry, this is contrary to the doctrine of the scriptures and to orthodox faith, is assuming a jurisdiction not given to any Lord Chancellor. As to Lord Eldon's orthodoxy, I give him full credit: like his wig, it belongs to his costume; but as to any religious opinion adopted upon mature examination and reflection, I would as soon give credit to one of his lordship's coach horses. He votes like Sir Robert Walpole's member, newly raised to the peerage, *as my Lords the Bishops do.*

Richard Carlisle, after this decision, published a very good edition of Lawrence's lectures, with the following dedication:

"This edition of these important lectures, is dedicated "to John, Earl of Eldon, Lord High Chancellor of "England, as the result of his injustice in refusing to es- "tablish the author's right of property in them, by the "publisher, 1823."

I know not a man living, more grossly and stupidly ignorant and bigoted, as to every question of liberal science and state policy, than Lord Eldon; whose departure from the ministry was justly regarded by the public as a national blessing. His predecessor, Lord Hardwicke, the father of the marriage act, was a man of the same stamp. The utter absurdity of his speech in defence of the corporation and test acts, as preserved in *Burgh's Political Disquisitions,* cannot be perused with a grave face. It must have been irresistibly ludicrous in the delivery.

His Lordship Eldon) gave the same decision afterwards, in the case of one of Lord Byron's publications. Lord Eldon is certainly one of the most efficient abettors of heresy and heterodoxy, that these errors have ever enlisted.

Mr. Lawrence, I believe, was afterwards re-elected as professor: no professional man being found to oppose him. The case forms a feature in the history of the times, and therefore I present it to the reader.

Mr. Lawrence was afterwards persuaded to write a letter to Sir Richard Carr Glynn, President of the Bridewell and Bethlehem Hospitals, April 16th, 1822, (see Monthly Magazine, June, 1822,) apologizing for the publication complained of, and for an argument which never has been, and never will be, refuted,—an argument which no anatomist, or physiologist, or physician, has yet attempted, or ever will attempt to refute. *Mr. Abernethy,* the great friend and defender of John Hunter's doctrine of vitality, disgraced himself by his opposition to Lawrence, who had been opposed to the notions of John Hunter; but though *Abernethy* was a time-serving bigot, he has been too wise to attempt meddling with a train of reasoning which he well knows can never be shaken.

The editor of the Monthly Magazine above cited, has given us the ABJURATION OF GALILEO, which, as it may entertain some of my readers, I copy as follows: "I, "GALILEO GALILEI, son of the late Vincent Galileo, a "Florentine, aged seventy, appearing personally in judg-

" ment, and being on my knees in the presence of you, " most eminent and most reverend Lords Cardinals of the " Universal Christian Commonwealth, Inquisitors-Gene- " eral against heretical depravity, having before my eyes " the holy gospels on which I now lay my hands, swear, " that I have always believed, and do now believe, and " God helping, that I shall in future always believe, what- " ever the Holy Catholic and Apostolic Roman Church " holds, preaches, and teaches. But because this holy office " had enjoined me, by precept, entirely to relinquish the " false dogma, which maintains that the sun is the centre " of the world and immoveable, and that the earth is not " the centre, and moves; not to hold, defend, or teach, " by any means or by writing, the aforesaid false doctrine: " and after it had been notified to me, that the aforesaid " doctrine is repugnant to the holy scripture; I have written " and printed a book in which I treat of the same doctrine " already condemned, and adduce reasons with great effi- " cacy in favor of it, not offering any solution of them; " therefore I have been adjudged and vehemently sus- " pected of heresy, namely, that I maintained and believed " that the sun is the centre of the world, and immoveable; " and that the earth is not the centre, and moves.

" Therefore, being willing to take out of the minds of " your Eminences and of every Catholic Christian this " vehement suspicion, of right conceived against me, I, " with sincere heart and faith unfeigned, abjure, execrate, " and detest the above said errors and heresies, and gene- " rally every other error and sect contrary to the above- " said Holy Church; and I swear that I will never more " hereafter say or assert, by speech or writing, any thing " through which the like suspicion may be had of me; " but if I shall know any one heretical or suspected of " heresy, I will denounce him to this holy office, or to " the Inquisitor or Ordinary of the place in which I shall " be. I moreover swear and promise that I will fulfil and " observe entirely all the penitences which have been im-

"posed upon, or which shall be imposed by this holy "office. But if it shall happen that I shall go contrary, "(which God avert,) to any of my words, promises, pro-"testations, or oaths, I subject myself to all the penalties "and punishments, which by the holy canons and other "constitutions, general and particular, have been enacted "and promulgated against such delinquents. So help me "God and his holy gospels, on which I now lay my hands.

"I, the aforesaid GALILEO GALILEI, have abjured, "sworn, promised, and have bound myself as above, and "in the fidelity of those declarations with my own hands; "and have subscribed to this present writing of my abju-"ration, which I have recited word by word, at Rome, "in the Convent of Minerva, this 22d June, of the year "1633. I, GALILEO GALILEI, have abjured, as above, "with my own hands."

The principal mover against Mr. Lawrence, appears to have been some person of the name of B. Burgess, of Highbury Park; whose name would be of no other consequence, except on Pope's principle,—"See Cromwell "damn'd to everlasting fame." It may be worth while to perpetuate, as far as possible, the contempt in which such a creature (still more excusable than Abernethy,) is deservedly held. I think Galileo was right not to offer up his life, as a sacrifice to the cruelty of these bigots. A man is not called upon to sacrifice his life or well being to the gratification of those whose aim is to effect, and who would rejoice at effecting his murder or his misery. It is a clear case of duress per minas. Suppose I were taken by an Algerine Corsair, and carried in as a slave. Suppose I was carried before the Dey, who, by his Drago-man, should address me, in the usual language of polite-ness of that humane and polished people. "Christian "dog! will you have your infidel foreskin circumcised, "and declare aloud that God is just, and Mahomet is his "prophet, and become a true believer? or will you prefer "to have three hundred bastinadoes on the soles of your

"feet, and then have an iron spike driven up your funda-
"ment, passing along side of your backbone on the inside
"of your body, and coming out at the nape of your neck?
"Christian dog! choose immediately."—I should say:
"Merciful commander of true believers! I am penetrated
"with your goodness; I will not give any servant of the
"prophet the great trouble of bastinadoing and impaling
"your humble and devoted slave. God is great, and Ma-
"homet is his prophet; and I am ready to undergo the
"rest of the ceremony." And why not? What obligation can I be under, to submit to be impaled for the amusement and gratification of such savages? Would the Almighty expect this as a duty from me, for no purpose whatever, but to excite the merriment of cruel and relentless persecutors, into whose merciless hands he has willed me to be thrown? The principle of duress per minas, holds out both for Galileo and Lawrence, a full justification.

In the year 1826, a similar persecution was instituted against a Mr. Macartney, lecturer in physiology and anatomy, at Dublin: what the result is, I know not. This I know, that since every physiologist of eminence, whose works are put into the hands of our students of medicine in Europe, and in this country, leans manifestly to the opinion that the intellectual phenomena are exclusively dependent on the properties of our nervous system as we find it organized, and the excitments by which it is brought into action, there will not be, in the course of ten years, one well informed physician in any part of the civilized world, who will hold a different opinion from that which has incurred the hostility of Mr. Burgess: it is well for this wiseacre, that he has no reputation to lose; for there is little chance of his retaining any that a man of common sense would not be glad to renounce. These fiery zealots are hastening their own downfall. In thus apologizing for what is called materialism, I advance no opinion but what I firmly believe is to be found in the Christian

Scriptures: and I hope I am guarantied in my honest construction of that rule of faith and doctrine, as much as my neighbor is in his.

The clergy of England have not been content with exhibiting their ignorant rancor against the doctrine of materialism, but they look with a very jealous eye, and cry down as much as they dare, the zoological disquisitions into the origin of the families of mankind, and the geological disquisitions into the present appearances and original formation of the state of the earth. I forbear to dwell on the carelessness or ignorance among the clergy of that country of what the Scriptures really contain. They are a class of men by no means pre-eminent for *useful* knowledge of any kind, and with some exceptions very deficient in biblical knowledge particularly. What need of it to them? They constitute *a church by law established.* They are a part of the political apparatus of that country. But if men of science are thus to be met at the threshold of their inquiries, by the threats of ignorance and bigotry, and subjected to persecution for an honest pursuit of mere scientific investigation, because it may possibly interfere with the prejudice or the interest of the clerical order:— if this I say is to be the case, it is high time to put that order down altogether, as an obstacle to the propagation of useful knowledge, and a nuisance in society, that the public ought to abate without scruple. They seem to be of opinion with the Mahomedan Caliph who burned the library of Alexandria. "If these books contain what the "Koran contains, they are useless: if they contain any "thing but what the Koran contains, they are pernicious; "let them be burnt."

APPENDIX. NO. II.

I HAVE already referred to Jeremy Bentham's "swear not at all." I have met with the *wise* decision of Judge De Saussure on the testimony of what the clergy would call an unbeliever; and with the *unwise* decision of Judge Story on a point of the same general character. I wish to make a few brief observations on them. In England, where they have a set of theological dogmata established by law, however absurd they may be, (and Heaven knows they are sufficiently so,) yet some excuse is to be made for a judge in that country, who decides in conformity to the established alliance between church and state. Not so in this. The constitution of South Carolina, article viii. declares, "that the free exercise and enjoyment of religious profession and worship, without discrimination or preference, shall for ever hereafter be allowed in this state to all mankind: provided, that the liberty of conscience thereby declared, shall not be so construed as to excuse acts of licentiousness; or justify practices inconsistent with the peace or safety of this state."

Now, if a witness can be worried by an ignorant counsel, and compelled by a court of law, suddenly, upon the spur of the occasion, and publicly in open court, to state his religious creed; how can this be termed the *free exercise* and *enjoyment* of religious profession? How can *that* be the free enjoyment of religious profession, which is liable to the compulsory and coercive mandate of a judge on the bench? If a witness chooses to submit to the common form of swearing or affirmation, no judge has a right, under this constitution, to put any further questions to him. The witness has voluntarily made himself amenable to the penalties of perjury, if he should tell a falsehood in his character of a witness; and that is enough. I hope therefore, in future, witnesses will treat any questions, as to their religious creed, with contempt, if put before taking the oath, or after having sworn or affirmed in the usual way, or before it. A witness does all the law can require of him, by submitting to the usual ceremonies: and a judge who would commit him for refusing to answer further, as to his creed, ought to be impeached. Any man whose conscience will not permit him to swear on the bible, may tender his affirmation. Judge Story is a good black letter-case lawyer. But he seems to me to forget, that the judges of an English court, goaded on by a national system of religious intolerance and political ignorance, are not the best examples to be followed by the judges of a republic, where the obligations of religion are left to a man's own conscience: and the laws of the country decline all interference between a man and his Maker. Punish the crime of perjury as severely as the offence requires, but do not make the seat of quarrel and litigation a theatre for religious ceremonies; or profanely intermix the things of this world with those of the next; or convert a judge, who has no peculiar pretensions to religious knowledge, into a parson and a preacher.

Then again,—the difficulties so manifestly involved in the practice, furnish an insuperable argument against it. Suppose a witness suspected of Atheism: consider the many reasonable doubts and distinctions which a witness would have a clear right to suggest. How complicated, for instance, and indefinite is the definition of a God! and how many Christians of one persuasion, would disagree to the tenets of the others, in this respect. To say nothing of the Jews, the Mahomedans, or the Hindoos; no two beings can be imagined more dissimilar than the God of the Calvinists and the God of the Unitarians. " The God of the Calvinistic Trinitarians, your God, (said Dr. Maxcey, my predecessor, one evening in my hearing, to the Reverend Mr. Th. Charlton Henry,) is my Devil. He had some reason for saying so.

Extract from "Two Hundred and nine days on the Continent," by Thomas Jefferson Hogg, v. 1. p. 232. "The more swearing, the more falsehood: truth is not inconsistent with a simple assertion: an oath is an invitation to use deceit and evasion: it was the invention of those who sought to deceive, or who had deceived so often that they could not hope to be believed without some new expedient: it was a confession that the sense of justice had no force; but the apprehension of the consequences of a terrible imprecation, might possibly act upon the vile deceiver. It was a base substitution of cowardly fear for honesty. It was degrading the mind of a man, a courageous and moral being, to the state of a timorous brute, that flies before the goad and trembles under the lash."

What is it we require in a witness? That his sense of the obligations of veracity shall be paramount in his mind. That he shall be able and willing to tell the truth fearlessly, without being deterred by any consequences. Under the present prejudices entertained by the public, a man who declares himself a Deist, an unbeliever in Christianity, or in the doctrine of a future state of rewards and punishments after this life, *must be* a fearless and honest truth-teller. No man but an honest and sincerely conscientious man, would make a confession in a court of justice, which would not only tend to degrade him there, but would expose him to the rancor of every bigot, would injure his own reputation among his neighbors, and destroy the fair prospects of success that he might entertain for himself and his family. A man whose regard for truth will induce him deliberately to run these risks, cannot be a dishonest man. He has all the good qualities that you can require of a witness, and those too in an eminent degree. No higher test of veracity can be offered or expected. Yet according to the present silly practice, such a man in England is legally disqualified from giving evidence. However important his testimony may be, no one has a right to call for it. An estate may be adjudicated to a rogue who speculates on the stern integrity of a witness against him; a witness who will not degrade himself by telling a falsehood in open court, and who will fearlessly and at all hazards, acknowledge himself an unbeliever! This may be law, according to some men's notions; but it is gross absurdity and detestable injustice. Mean while, another man who cares not a cent about religion, acknowledges readily all the lies necessary to qualify him to become a legal witness, and is heard and believed without an investigation or objection. The character of the first man may have been not only unimpeached but highly praiseworthy, during the course of a long life: yet may his honest doubts and scruples disqualify him, as the law is now construed; while an abandoned professor of religion, or a nominal Christian (who never gave the subject one moment's serious thought,) is credited without hesitation! The evil I think, is and will be coeval with a hired and paid priesthood. Suppose a clergyman to be inducted into a valuable church living, to declare (as in England they do declare,) solemnly before God, that he is inwardly *moved by the Holy Ghost*, to enter upon the service of the ministry; (and what clergyman scruples this?) is such a man worthy of credit, upon any point where he, or his interest, or his family, or his profession, or the esprit du corps of the clerical order is in any way concerned? Does any human creature doubt for a moment but that he is moved by the income he expects to receive? A clergyman, it seems, may lie before God without scruples, and be regarded as a most holy man and an unimpeachable witness, while an honest unbeliever is not allowed to tell the truth, as to himself, with impunity, however necessary to legal justice his testimony may be!

So much for the "march of mind!" and this folly is the law of the land in Great Britain; in the most civilized country upon earth—in the year 1828! Would to God some contrivance could be discovered to civilize their judges and their parsons! who seem to consider truth as a crime and hypocrisy as a virtue; who substitute law for wisdom; and who have all kind of sense but *common sense*, and all kind of honesty but common honesty!

OATHS AND AFFIRMATIONS.

[From the New-York Enquirer, Jan. 1828.]

WE have lately had considerable discussion in Rhode Island relative to the admissibility of testimony from persons called *infidels*, and indeed the question is constantly presenting itself in some shape or other.

On the 29th ult. an action of trover was brought in the Marine Court, before Judge Scott.

On behalf of the plaintiff, a gentleman, a member of the *New-York Free Press Association*, was produced to give testimony, but was objected to by counsel for defendant, on the ground that he did not believe in a God, nor in a future state of rewards and punishments.

The judge interfered and questioned the legal propriety of interrogating the witness upon matters appertaining to any particular creed or religious belief; and as a sanction for this opinion, he quoted several eminent law authorities and late decisions regarding the admission of evidence from witnesses who might entertain opinions probably similar to those of the present witness, and the law went even so far as to say, that those termed infidels, who held to the solemn obligation and inviolability of an oath, were clearly admissible as evidence.

The counsel for the defendant again urged, that notwithstanding these authorities, they could not see how they applied to the present witness, for they were ready to produce evidence that this gentleman's philosophy taught him to deny the existence of a God altogether, and also a future state of rewards and punishments; and he has in an especial manner, avowed his entire disbelief in the God of Moses.

The counsel for the plaintiff here argued upon the various points in the law authorities and decisions already quoted, and also respecting the undoubted veracity of the witness, whose affirmation ought and must be admitted as sufficient evidence in this cause, or in any cause.

The counsel for the defendant frankly admitted the veracity of the witness, and from what they knew of the gentleman, they would as soon take his simple affirmation as the oath of any one. They expressed no further interest in the question, than being pressed to urge the objection by their client.

From some suggestions thrown out by the judge, at the instigation of the counsel, the witness obtained permission to state his opinions of a God, and a future state of rewards and punishments.

He believed, he said, in a great, powerful, and immutable ruling principle, inherent in the whole of nature, and this may be said to govern the universe. He cared not, neither did he consider it of any importance, whether this spirit or principle was denominated God, or by any other appellation. As to his opinions of a future state of rewards and punishments, he considered this subject of so abstruse and complicated a nature, as might tend to a high *philosophical* discussion, that perhaps would not be in accordance with the regular proceedings of this or any other court of justice. Regarding the solemn obligation of an oath, he had no hesitation to say, that a false oath or affirmation, being an evil act, would carry with it, or produce its own punishment, as virtue has its own reward; and this punishment might be said to be during the present or any future state of existence. He expressed an inclination to go no further on the present occasion; when the court asked him if he had scruples to swear upon the bible. He replied in the affirmative. His *affirmation* was accordingly taken as *legal testimony* in the cause.

APPENDIX. NO. III.

MR. JEFFERSON'S LETTER.

[From the Columbia Telescope, South Carolina.]

MR. EDITOR—The following letter was first published in England, in a paper called the London Nation, July 19, 1824, and thence copied into the Boston Daily Advertiser, of September 7, 1824. Since the death of *Major Cartwright*, who for more than half a century was the strenuous advocate of a parliamentary reform, it has been published among the documents connected with his life.

I have examined the Year Book cited. The passage is to be found in the case of Humphrey Bohun against John Broughton, Bishop of Lincoln, and others, a suit for disturbance in refusing to induct Thomas Young, presented by Bohun to the living of Holborne, in the county of Middlesex. The Bishop pleads, that on the same day another claimant, to wit, John Brown, had presented *his* clerk, Richard Ewenson. That the law of the Holy Church in such case is, that until the contest be decided by judgment on inquisition in a suit de jure patronatus, (on the right of presentation,) the ordinary is not bound to admit. And that it is the duty of the two contending patrons to institute such a suit, and not the duty of the ordinary. This not having been done within six months, it becomes the duty of the ordinary to *present*, that there may be no vacancy. The sentence quoted is Prisot's opinion, in page 40. b. of the Year Book. The translation of the passage is as follows: "*To such law as the Holy "Church hath under ancient record* (that is preserved in "old books; the French of holy scripture, is not ancient "scripture, but *sainte* ecriture,) *it becometh us to give "credence; for this is common law*, (that is, this consti- "tutes the common law of the church,) *upon which com- "mon law all other laws are founded: and so, sir, we "are bound to acknowledge the law of the holy church; "and in like manner they are bound to acknowledge our "law. And, sir, if it may appear to us that the bishop "has acted as an ordinary would have acted in like case, "we ought to acknowledge it as good, otherwise not.*"

To be sure, this dictum of HALE is founded either on gross ignorance, or on downright fraud and falsehood; for he had no other authority for it than the above passage, which cannot be read without surprise at its having been relied on for the purpose to which it has been converted.

The common law of England reaches back as far as the Saxon times. (See the opinions of the judges in the great case of literary property, Sir W. Blackstone's Rep.) It has been digested at various times in the laws of Ina, in the Leges Anglo-Saxonicæ, in the laws of King Alfred, and of Edward the Confessor. In the Anglo-Saxon times, the holy church was *Pagan;* in Prisot's time it was *Papist;* in the present time it is *Protestant;* and its doctrines are contained in the Athanasian creed, which King George the Third would never consent to repéat or respond to. A year or two ago a petition was presented to the House of Commons of Great Britain, signed by upwards of 2,000 members of the Church of England, many of them clergymen, praying that all prosecutions in defence of Christianity might be dropped; *inasmuch* as they appeared in the character of persecution for conscientious difference of opinion; *inasmuch* as the advocates of Christianity, in and out of the church, receiving salaries for defending and teaching Christianity, were and ought to be deemed quite competent to the defence of it; *inasmuch* as fact and argument ought to be opposed by fact and argument, and not by pains and penalties, by fine and imprisonment;

inasmuch as these prosecutions led to the injurious and ill founded suspicion that Christianity could not be supported in the field of free discussion; and finally, *inasmuch* as these prosecutions produced an effect directly opposite to that which was intended, increasing the number of obnoxious publications, operating as advertisements to make them more known, and exciting thousands to peruse them who would never have meddled with the controversy otherwise.

These remonstrances seem to have had the desired effect in England, upon the ministers of that country; for in consequence of a petition brought up by Mr. Brougham, on the 30th June, 1825, on the part of Richard Carlisle, who had been condemned to six years imprisonment and fined £1500 sterling. The fine was remitted in toto, and he was discharged. This was as it should be, for his influence arose only from his imprisonment. The outcry of persecution was raised, and the enemies of Christianity made the most of it. Christianity needs no protection but its own intrinsic truth, and the manifest superiority of the morality taught in the Gospels. If old objections are vamped up as new, reply to them by the republication of the old arguments by which they were heretofore refuted; and do not let it be suspected, that truths so useful, and so manifest, need any defence but their own evidence, and their own good tendency. X.

The following letter from the late President Jefferson, is found in "The "Life and Correspondence," (just published in England,) of the late Major Cartwright.

Monticello, in Virginia, June 5, 1824.

Dear and Venerable Sir—I am much indebted for your kind letter of February 29, and for your valuable volume on the English Constitution. I have read this with pleasure and much approbation; and I think it has deduced the constitution inherited by the English nation, from its rightful root, the Anglo-Saxon. It is really wonderful that so many able men should have failed in their attempts to define it with correctness; no wonder then that Paine, who thought more than he read, should have credited the great authorities who have declared that the will of Parliament is the Constitution of England. So Marbois, before the French revolution, observed to me, that the Almanac Royal wås the Constitution of France. Your derivation of it from the Anglo-Saxons, seems to be made on legitimate principles. Having driven out the former inhabitants of that part of the island called England, they became, as to you, aborigines, and your lineal ancestors. They doubtless had a constitution; and although they have not left it in a written formula, to the precise text of which you may always appeal, yet they have left fragments of their history and laws, from which it may be inferred with considerable certainty. Whatever their history and laws show to have been practised with approbation, we may presume was permitted by their constitution; whatever was not so practised was not permitted; and although this constitution was violated and set at nought by Norman force, yet force cannot change right; a perpetual claim was kept up by the nation in their perpetual demand of the restoration of their Saxon laws, which shows they never were relinquished by the will of the nation. In the pullings and haulings for these ancient rights, between the nation and its kings of the races of Plantagenets, Tudors, and Stuarts, there was sometimes gain and sometimes loss, until the final reconquest of their rights from the Stuarts broke the thread of pretended inheritance, extinguished all regal usurpations, and the nation re-entered into all its rights: and although in their bill of rights they specifically reclaim some only, yet the omission of others was no renunciation of the right to assume their exercise also, whenever occasions should occur. The new king received no rights or powers but those expressly granted to him. It has ever appeared to me, that the difference between the whig and the tory of England, is, that the whig deduces his rights from the

Anglo-Saxon source, the tory from the Norman: and Hume, the great apostle of toryism, says, in so many words, (note as to chap. 42.) "that in the reigns of the Stu- "arts, it was the people who encroached upon the sove- "reign, not the sovereign who attempted, as is pretend- "ed, to usurp upon the people;" this supposes the Norman usurpations to be rights in his successors; and again, (c. 59.) "the commons established a principle, which is "noble in itself, and seems specious, but is belied from "all history and experience, *that the people are the origin* "*of all JUST power!*" And where else will this degenerate son of science, this traitor to his fellow-men, find the origin of just power, if not in the majority of the society? Will it be in the majority of the society? Will it be in the minority, or in an individual of that minority?

Our revolution commenced on more favorable ground. It presented us an album, on which we were free to write what we pleased; we had no occasion to search into musty records, to hunt up royal parchments, or to investigate the laws and institutions of a semi-barbarous ancestry. We appealed to those of nature, and found them engraved in our hearts, yet we did not avail ourselves of all the advantages of our position. We had never been permitted to exercise self-government: when forced to assume it, we were novices in its science; its principles and forms had entered little into our former education; we established, however, some, although not all, of its important principles. The constitutions of most of our states assert, that all power is inherent in the people; that they may exercise it by themselves, in all cases to which they think themselves competent; (as in electing their functionaries, executive and legislative, and deciding by a jury of themselves both fact and law, in all judiciary cases in which any fact is involved;) or they may act by representatives, freely and equally chosen: that it is their right and duty to be at all times armed; that they are entitled to freedom of person, freedom of religion, freedom of property, and freedom of the press. In the structure of our legislatures, we think experience has proved the benefit of subjecting questions to two separate bodies of deliberants; but in constituting these, natural right has been mistaken; some making one of these bodies, and some both, the representatives of property instead of persons, whereas the double deliberation might be as well obtained without any violation of true principle, either by requiring a greater age in one of the bodies, or by electing a proper number of representatives of persons, dividing them by lot into two chambers, and renewing the division at frequent intervals, in order to break up cabals.

Virginia, of which I am myself a native and resident, was not only the first of the states, but I believe I may say, the first of the nations of the earth, which assembled its wise men peaceably together to form a fundamental constitution, to commit it to writing, and place it among their archives, where every one should be free to appeal to its text. But this act was very imperfect; the other states, as they proceeded successively to the same work, made successive improvements, and several of them, still further corrected by experience, have by conventions, still further amended their first forms. My own state has gone on so far with its *premiere ebauche*, but it is now proposing to call a convention for amendment. Among other improvements, I hope they will adopt the sub-divisions of our counties into wards; the former may be estimated at an average of twenty-four miles square, the latter should be six miles square, each, and would answer to the hundreds of your Saxon Alfred. In each of these might be, 1. An elementary school; 2. A company of militia, with its officers; 3. A justice of the peace and a constable; 4. Each ward should take care of their own poor; 5. Of their own roads; 6. Their own police; 7. Elect within themselves, one or more jurors to attend the courts of justice; 8. And here give in at their folk-house their votes for all functionaries reserved to their election.

Each ward would thus be a small republic within itself, and every man in the state would thus become an acting member in the common government, transacting in person a great portion of its rights and duties, subordinate indeed, but important, and entirely within his competence. The wit of man cannot devise a more solid basis for a free, durable, and well administered republic.

With respect to our state and federal governments, I do not think their regulations correctly understood by foreigners. They generally suppose the former subordinate to the latter; but this is not the case, they are co-ordinate departments of one simple integral whole. To the state governments are reserved all legislation and administration in affairs which concern their own citizens only; and to the federal government is given whatever concerns foreigners, or the citizens of other states. These functions alone being federal, the one is the domestic, the other the foreign branches of the same government; neither having control over the other, but within its own department. There are one or two exceptions only to this partition of power. But, you may ask, if the two departments should claim each the same subject of power, where is the common umpire to decide ultimately between them. In cases of little importance or urgency, the prudence of both parties will keep them aloof from the questionable ground; but if it can neither be avoided nor compromised, a convention of the states must be called, to ascribe the doubtful power to that department which they may think best. You will perceive by these details, that we have not so far perfected our constitutions as to venture to make them unchangeable; but still, in their present state, we consider them not otherwise changeable than by the immediate authority of the people, or a special election of representatives for that purpose expressly. They are till then the lex legum.

But can they be made unchangeable? Can one generation bind another, and all others in succession for ever?

I think not. The Creator hath made the earth for the living, not the dead. Rights and powers can only belong to persons, not to things; not to mere matter unendowed with will: the dead are not even things. The particles of matter which compose their bodies make part now of the bodies of other animals, vegetables, or minerals of a thousand forms. To what then are attached the rights and powers they held while in the form of man? A generation may bind itself as long as its majority continues in life. When that has disappeared, another majority is in place, holds all the rights and powers their predecessors once held, and may change their laws and institutions to suit themselves: nothing then is unchangeable but the inherent and unalienable rights of man.

I was glad to find in your book a formal contradiction, at length, of the judiciary usurpation of legislative powers; for such the judges have usurped, in their repeated decisions that Christianity is a part of the common law. The proof of the contrary, which you have adduced, is incontrovertible, to wit, that the common law existed while the Anglo-Saxons were yet Pagans; at a time when they had never yet heard the name of Christ pronounced, or knew that such a character had existed. But it may amuse you to show when and by what means they stole this law upon us. In a case quare impedit, in the Year Book, 34 H. 6. fo. 38. (1453,) a question was made, how far the ecclesiastical law was to be respected in a common law court? And Prisot, c. 5. gives his opinion in these words: " A tielx Leis que ils de Saint Eglise ont en *ancien scripture*, covient a nous a doner credence; car ceo Common Ley sur quel touts maus Leis sont fondes. Et auxy sir, nous sumus obliges de conustre lout Ley de Saint Egl', et semblablement ils sont obliges de conustre nostre Ley. Et sir, si poit apperer or a nous que l'evesque ad fait come un ordinary fera en tiel cas, adonq nous devons ceo adjuger bon, ou autermcnt nemy," &c. See S. C. Fitzh. Abr. qu. imp. 89; Bro. Abr. qu. imp. 12. Finch, in his first book, c. 3.

is the first, afterwards, who quotes this case, and misstates it thus: " To such laws of the church as have warrant in *holy scripture*, our law giveth credence;" and cites Prisot, mis-translating " ancient scripture," into " holy scripture;" whereas Prisot palpably says, " to such laws as those of holy church have in *ancient writing*, it is proper for us to give credence;" to wit, to their ancient written laws. This was in 1613, a century and a half after the dictum of Prisot. Wingate, in 1658, erects this false translation into a maxim of the common law, copying the words of Finch, but citing Prisot. Wingate, max. 3, and Sheppard, tit. " religion," in 1675, copies the same mis-translation, quoting the Y. B. Finch, and Wingate. Hale expresses it in these words: " Christianity is parcel of the laws of England," 1 Ventr. 293; 3 Keb. 607; but quotes no authority. By these echoings and re-echoings, from one to another, it had become so established in 1728, that in the case of the King v. Woolston, 2 Stra. 834. the court would not suffer it to be debated, whether to write against Christianity was punishable in the temporal courts at common law? Wood, therefore, 409. ventures still to vary the phrase, and says " that all blasphemy and profaneness are offences by the common law," and cites 2 Stra.; then Blackstone, in 1763, IV. 59. repeats the words of Hale, that Christianity is part of the common law of England, citing Ventris and Strange; and finally Lord Mansfield, with a little qualification, in Evan's case, in 1767, says " that the essential principles of revealed religion are parts of the common law," thus engulphing bible, testament, and all, into the common law, without citing any authority. And thus far we find this chain of authorities hanging, link by link, one upon another, and all ultimately upon one and the same hook, and that a mis-translation of the words " ancient scripture," used by Prisot. Finch quotes Prisot; Wingate does the same; Sheppard quotes Prisot, Finch, and Wingate; Hale cites nobody; the court, in Woolston's case, cites Hale; Wood cites Woolston's case; Blackstone quotes Woolston's case, and Hale, and Lord Mansfield, like Hale, ventures it on his own authority. Here I might defy the best read lawyer to produce another scrip of authority for this *judiciary forgery;* and I might go on further to show how some of the Anglo-Saxon clergy interpolated into the text of Alfred's laws, the 20th, 21st, 22d, and 23d chapters of Exodus, and the 15th of the Acts of the Apostles, from the 23d to the 29th verses. But this would lead my pen and your patience too far. What a conspiracy this, between church and state!!! Sing tantararara, rogues all; rogues all; sing tantararara, rogues all!

I must still add to this long and rambling letter, my acknowledgements for your good wishes to the university we are now establishing in this state. There are some novelties in it; of that of a professorship of the principles of government, you express your approbation. They will be founded in the rights of man: that of agriculture I am sure you will approve; and that also of Anglo-Saxon. As the histories and laws left us, in that type and dialect must be the text books of the reading of the learners: they will imbibe with the language their free principles of government. The volumes you have been so kind as to send, shall be placed in the library of the university. Having at this time, in England, a person sent for the purpose of selecting some professors, (a Mr. Gilmer of my neighborhood,) I cannot but recommend him to your patronage, counsel, and guardianship, against imposition, misinformation, and the deceptions of partial and false recommendations, in this selection of characters; he is a gentleman of great worth and correctness, my particular friend, well educated in various branches of science, and worthy of entire confidence.

Your age of eighty-four and mine of eighty-one years, ensures us a speedy meeting. We may then comment at leisure, and more fully, on the good and evil which, in the course of our long lives, we have both witnessed; and in the mean time, I pray you to accept assurances of my high veneration and esteem for your person and character.

THOMAS JEFFERSON.